Welcome to *Airlock*!

Airlock is a
that contair
undated mc
whenever yc
like. There ar
five daily note
the weekend
it in the way that benefits you the
most.

es systematically through
oks of the Bible. This is
ook in the series,
ou don't have to read
order.

This issue we **start looking at the story of Isaac**, and continue our voyages through the books of **Psalms, Isaiah, Obadiah, Zephaniah, Matthew, Acts** and **1 Corinthians**.

Each daily page is divided into three sections:

Decompress

This is a short prayer or thought designed to get you in the right frame of mind to read the Bible, and to prepare you for what you're about to read. After the Decompress section, you'll be given the Bible passage for the day. It doesn't matter what Bible version you use – just make sure you open up your Bible!

Immerse

This section contains ways of relating the Bible passage to today's culture. It also explains anything difficult in the Bible passage, and will help you understand the context the passage was written in.

Re-engage

This section encourages you to take what you've learned from the Bible passage and apply it to your day-to-day life through practical suggestions and pointers.

Step into the *Airlock* and relieve the pressure!

Written by Jenny Baker (D/56–60), Andy Brown (D/21–25), Andrew Cupples (D/26–30), Lizzie Green (D/06–10), Darren Hill (D/41–45), Howard Ingham (D/36–40), Nick Lear (D/11–15), James Lovelock (D/31–35, D/46–50), Ruth McCaughren (D/01–05), Al Rodgers (D/16–20), Robin Rolls (D/51–55) and Steve Tilley (D/61–65)

Edited by Andrew Cupples, Lizzie Green and Darren Hill.

Designed and illustrated by Martin Lore. Cover photography by Chris Brown.

Airlock: **Dedicated**

Is it all about the bling?

D/01

Decompress

Have you told a whopper of a lie recently or even a little one? Take a moment to think about what you have said today – was it all true and good for those who heard it? Did it point to Jesus?

>'Father, thank you for the truth, and help me to speak it all the time. Amen.'

Now read Acts 5:1–11

Immerse

Imagine that a boy is about to propose to his girlfriend. The question eventually comes – 'Will you marry me?' – and out comes the ring from his pocket. But things go wrong. The boy says it's diamond and platinum and it's cost him a small fortune, but the girl can see it's only silver and plastic. And she's very upset.

>Is the girl upset because she didn't want to marry him? Or because he's proposed to her on the back of a bus? No, she's shocked that he thinks it is appropriate to lie at that crucial, all-or-nothing moment. She doesn't care what the ring is made of, but why bother lying to make the gift sound better?

>Ananias and Sapphira lied to God; they made their gift seem a much bigger sacrifice than it actually was to them. Being real with God is so important; we need to be truthful with God and that means also being true to all that God has made, ie other humans!

Re-engage

As Christians, our actions are crucial to how others see Jesus. If you lie, cheat and deceive others, people won't be attracted to see Jesus as the Truth. Our actions and words need to point to God, so more people can know him.

>Perhaps today could be a day when you're completely honest with God about your money. Give some to your church or a local charity… it doesn't have to be much, but it matters how you give – don't do it because you have to, or because I've told you to even, but do it because you want to.

>It might help you to give willingly to God to think about all the things that he has given willingly to you!

Airlock: Dedicated

Follow your leader?

D/02

Decompress

Being a Christian is sometimes a real challenge – maybe your friends have teased you recently for your faith. Pray that your faith might grow, so that you might be a stronger person for Christ.

Now read Acts 5:12–24

Immerse

I have just finished university. University is a tricky place to be – away from home, with everything you could imagine available for you to experience. One thing I was sure of when I went to uni was that I had to let people know that I was a Christian. I lived in a house of people who weren't Christians at all. Most of the time they were cool with what I believed, but I remember one occasion when they were not.

>I'd been to a Christian Union event and rushed home to go out with them to a club. On the way to the club they started to talk about my beliefs and how ridiculous they were, and why on earth I would want to work for a Christian organisation? I felt hurt, persecuted and let down. So much so, that as soon as we arrived I jumped into a taxi and went home.

>Looking back on that night now, I realise that they felt threatened by my beliefs and didn't want to recognise God in the things that my life was about. When you are true to your faith in your relationships with your friends, they notice. When the Holy Spirit starts working through you, people feel challenged because they notice something different.

Re-engage

I know that God has used me with my uni friends to show them something of him. When you get persecuted, just like the early church apostles did, sometimes life seems impossible and not great. But the apostles were full of joy because they obeyed God, even though they experienced real pain and oppression. Hearing God's command to love him and follow him is the toughest but the best thing you can do with your life. Don't give up!

>Write a list of all your friends and people that you know. Start praying for the ones who don't know God, that the Holy Spirit might give you opportunities to share with them about your faith. Be prepared to be knocked for your faith, and pray that God might strengthen you for it. Check out 1 Peter 1:3–9.

Airlock: Dedicated

The joy of wax

D/03

Decompress

What do your friends think about you being a Christian? Is it funky, or a not-so-cool topic for discussion? Pray that God will show you ways in which you can be bold and joyful about sharing your faith, especially when its hard.

Now read Acts 5:25–42

Immerse

Most people don't like pain, grief or suffering. But are there some things you would do, even if they caused you grief?

>The book of Acts is an amazing account of what the first Christians went through because of their love of Christ, and of their unquenchable desire to tell other people about what Jesus had done for them, often at great personal cost to themselves.

>Here, Peter and John have just been released from prison and have been taken to the high court for talking about Jesus. Most of us would see this as a time to be quiet and not cause a fuss. Peter, on the other hand, uses this as an opportunity to tell the high priest the good news about Jesus forgiving all our sins! They are released thanks to some wise words from Gamaliel and then beaten heavily. Most people would react in horror if they were beaten up for their faith. But not the disciples – they were full of joy! Why? Because they had been given the honour of suffering disgrace for Jesus. I'm completely challenged by this. If Peter could be joyful at being in prison and receiving a beating, the challenges I face seem small – how about you?

Re-engage

Actively seek out some information about Christians around the world who are persecuted because of their faith in Christ. Perhaps you know of some missionaries from your church, working in countries where Christians suffer and get put in prison for God. Pray for them that they may know Gods peace and joy, and that their oppressors might release them soon.

>You could try going online and checking out www.opendoorsuk.org for a start.

Airlock: Dedicated

Ripple, ripple?

Decompress

Thank God that he gives us a part to play in his plan. Pray that he will show you what he wants you to do now and in the future for him.

Now read Acts 6:1–7

Immerse

I work for the YMCA in East London. I'd like to tell you about one woman who had a good idea. She noticed a homeless person near to where she lived who was hungry, so the next day she brought him some food. She kept doing it almost every night. Soon he brought some friends along, and it became known that there was a lady who made great food for those who wanted it. She then realised she couldn't feed all the hungry people in East London, so she asked for help at her church. And they still kept coming. So the church approached the YMCA and now this small idea has a proper van, kitchens, staff, over 200 volunteers, even government funding – and feeds about 70 people every night, 365 days a year.

>This lady had discovered that for her great idea to become what God wanted it to be, more people needed to be involved in running the project, so that more hungry people could be fed.

Re-engage

Everyone has a part to play in God's plan. The apostles needed more people involved so they could do what they were called to do. 1 Corinthians 12:12 talks about the body having many parts – all equal, all needed. The most persuasive reason to work like this is that when we as Christians work together, the effect multiplies. Like dropping a stone in a pond, ripples start to flow out – the bigger the stones, the bigger the ripples.

>Take a piece of paper and a pen, and write down everything you do; playing an instrument, working hard, being a good a listener, helping out at church etc and thank God that you are able to do lots of things. Then take a long, hard look at your list and make sure you are doing the things you are gifted at, rather than the things that just need to be done. Everyone should use their gifts to serve God and be happy that their part is equal in God's sight.

Hands up for botox?

D/05

Decompress

Go find a mirror, and look at your face. What do you see? What do others see? Pray that your faith in Christ might shine through your face.

Now read Acts 6:8–15

Immerse

We live in a society obsessed with image. The other day I caught myself saying in the mirror to my 23-year-old face 'maybe it's time for some botox'. Now, obviously it is exceptionally worrying that I talk to myself in the mirror, but it's even more worrying that our culture is suggesting – and I'm accepting – that I should have my forehead injected with muscle freeze rather than having wrinkles.

>Our culture says our face is very important, and it is, but maybe not for the reasons that the world thinks.

>What does your face look like? What does it say about you? If someone who'd never met you saw a photo of your face for the first time, what do you think they'd say about you?

Re-engage

Stephen was an incredibly impressive man – he obeyed God, he spread the good news, he said all the right things, he was full of the Holy Spirit, he was fearless... But he also got on the wrong side of the Jewish leaders, who didn't like being outwitted and out-argued. So they put him on trial – an innocent man being tried for a crime he didn't commit.

>Stephen's face is described as like that of an angel's (v 15). I'm not sure what an angel's face would look like, but I imagine it's good. Stephen's face pointed to God. Can you see God glowing through your skin?

>Take a picture of yourself with a camera. Get the picture processed or download it from your camera and print it out. Stick it in your Bible. Write near it 'Does my face shine with God's glory?' Pray for help to develop your faith, that it might shine like a light leading others to Christ.

Airlock: Dedicated

Think about the things you've
given to God recently. Make a list of
them here…

1 _____
2 _____
3 _____
4 _____
5 _____
6 _____
7 _____
8 _____
9 _____
10 _____

How do they hold up? Are your gifts
to God a bit of a joke?

Extra_1 Deuteronomy 26:1–11
Extra_2 Luke 11:37–44

Take it easy

D/06

Decompress

Relax all your muscles. Take a few deep breaths. Feel the tension leave your body. Clear your mind of anything that's worrying you. Be still. Now, listen to God.

Now read Matthew 11:25–30

Immerse

I think too much. That's my problem. I lay awake at night, going over the details of my day, replaying conversations, thinking of the things I wished I'd said or done. Or I think through my plans for the next day, week or month. I can't switch off my thoughts, I can't sleep.

>Sometimes, I need to consciously clear my mind of all my thoughts in order to find rest. And it's often only then, with an open mind, that I can hear God.

>It's not that Jesus doesn't want us to use our brains, just that sometimes our thoughts and preconceptions can get in the way of meeting with God. During his life on earth, the people who accepted Jesus' teaching were generally not the wise and learned, but the poor, the sick, the shepherds, the fishermen. By simply following Jesus and spending time with him, they discovered more about God than years of studying the scriptures would have taught them.

Re-engage

Life is hard work. We have to deal with all sorts of stresses and strains every day. Relationships breaking down, exam pressure, illness… And becoming a Christian doesn't provide an escape from all this. In fact, it can often make things worse. Jesus warns us of this himself (John 16:33).

>But there is good news in this passage. Jesus doesn't promise to take away all our problems, but he does promise to help us deal with them. If we allow him to take our heavy load onto his shoulders, he will give us rest in return.

>If you find it hard to clear your mind of distractions and to be still before God, you could try using 'The Jesus Prayer', one of the earliest Christian prayers.

>Find a quiet place, on your own. Get yourself into a comfortable position. Slow your breathing and concentrate on each breath. Then, begin to say the prayer in your head. As you breathe in say, 'Lord Jesus Christ'. As you breathe out say, 'Have mercy on me'. Continue in this way until you feel uncomfortable or your mind begins to wander.

>At first it might seem strange, but it gets easier the more often you do it. Try using the prayer to unwind at the end of a stressful day.

Airlock: Dedicated

Full of it

Decompress

'Jesus, help me today to make you Lord of my life, in everything that I do and say. Help me to know more of who you are. Amen.'

Now read Matthew 12:1–14

Immerse

Do you know any Christians who are really full of themselves? Maybe they play guitar in the worship band and act like they're the next Tim Hughes. Or maybe their parents are missionaries and they think that makes them spiritually superior to everyone else.

>The Pharisees were a bit like that. They thought they were the best kind of Jews and the only ones who truly kept all of God's laws. And they didn't want an outspoken carpenter from Nazareth showing them up – especially not one who said that he was greater than the Temple and had the authority to override the Sabbath laws.

>The Pharisees were so concerned about obeying every one of God's laws, and criticising people who didn't keep them, that they failed to see God when he was standing right in front of them.

>Whether you go to a high Anglican church or a lively house church, you'll find it has rules and traditions. They may not always be carved in stone, but they will be there. And it's amazing how much fuss some people will make if you try to change them – 'But we've always done it this way!'

Re-engage

I'm not saying that rules aren't important. Some are the God-given foundations of the church. But what Jesus was trying to show the Pharisees was that they shouldn't forget who had given them the Law in the first place – God. And listening to God's voice, and obeying him, would always be more important than religiously keeping every law just because that was the way it had always been done.

>God gave his people laws to help them, but they had given the Law more authority than God in their lives. By letting his disciples eat when they were hungry, and healing the man whose hand was crippled, Jesus showed that God's first concern was for people, not strict application of the Law.

>Think about your group of friends, your youth group, your church. Is there something that you do, because you've always done it, which has become more important than the needs of the people involved? Ask God to show you what's important to him.

Airlock: Dedicated

Hope actually

D/08

Decompress

Seen the news today? Was any of it good? Didn't think so. Fortunately, there's plenty of good news in today's reading.

Now read Matthew 12:15–21

Immerse

Watching the news or reading a newspaper can often leave me feeling really depressed – war, terrorism, serial killers, the continuing spread of disease and poverty… It's enough to make anyone lose hope.

>All those in power, whether they are in charge of corporations or continents, seem blinkered and ignorant, only caring about getting more money, more land, more security, more status, and they're prepared to fight and kill to get it. The voices of those who work for peace and justice always seem to get drowned out. The loudest and the strongest always win.

>But thousands of years before Jesus was born, Isaiah knew there was another way to victory. A better way. Ultimately, the only way. The Messiah, the Servant – Jesus. It is only by trusting in him, and following his way of humility and compassion, that we can continue to have hope for a just and peaceful world.

Re-engage

Jesus was the promised Messiah, the Son of God, the Saviour – and yet his ministry was often so low-key that it must have baffled his followers. Many of them believed that the Messiah would come to liberate them from the Romans and establish a new Jewish kingdom that would be the envy of the world. In Jesus, they hoped for a great warrior-king.

>But Jesus' power was in his humility, his compassion, his love for the weak and the poor. In this passage he avoids a confrontation with the Pharisees and continues to heal the sick, trying to keep his identity concealed rather than shouting it from the rooftops. His main concern was always for people, not worldly status or power. And that is why he was willing to give up everything, even his life, to save those people he loved.

>Get hold of a newspaper, or check out the BBC online news page. It won't take you long to find a situation which seems hopeless, a story where injustice rules. Take some time to read the facts and focus on the issues involved.

>Then bring the situation to God. Ask him to bring hope where there is none, and to restore his perfect justice.

Airlock: Dedicated

Decisions, decisions

D/09

Decompress

'Father God, I have so many choices to make each day, I'm scared I'll make the wrong decision. But I know I made the right decision to follow you, And today, I choose to make that decision count.'

Now read Matthew 12:22–37

Immerse

Some people don't consciously reject God, they just put off making a decision. They figure they've got plenty of time to think about it. But sometimes they haven't. And it's too late. Jesus says, 'Whoever is not with me is against me.' He doesn't mention all those people who are still sitting on the fence.

>Jesus' warning about the 'unforgivable sin' can sound quite scary. How do we know if we've done it? Why won't he forgive us? But it's important to read this in context. Jesus is warning us not to look at the work of the Holy Spirit and say that Satan is responsible. By doing this we give Satan more power, and cut ourselves off from God's forgiveness. Forgiveness comes through the Spirit, and we cannot receive it if we do not believe in the Spirit's power.

>So the warning is serious, but we shouldn't get too worried about it. If you're worried about committing this sin, it probably means you won't! But it does leave us all with an important decision to make. If Jesus was working in God's power, then he must have been who he said he was. Refusing to recognise this truth means cutting yourself off from God, and from his forgiveness.

Re-engage

'The mouth speaks the things that are in the heart. Good people have good things in their hearts, and so they say good things.'

>It's easy to say horrible things without really thinking about it; to insult someone, to make someone feel small, to tell a crude or insensitive joke. But Jesus says that we are responsible for every careless thing that we say.

>Take your responsibility seriously. Is there anything in your life that is filling your mind with rubbish? It could be the people you hang around with, the films you watch or the music you listen to. How much time do you spend doing those things? Try to spend as much, if not more, time with God – reading your Bible, praying, worshipping with other Christians. Fill your heart with good things. And always think before you speak.

Airlock: Dedicated

'Who do you say I am?'

Decompress

'... Jesus asked, "But who do you say I am?" (Luke 9:20).

Now read Matthew 12:38–45

Immerse

Jesus' story about the evil spirits is a serious warning against half-hearted repentance. Getting rid of the wrong things in your life is only half the story; if you don't then fill that void with the good things of God, then there is room for the wrong things to return. This is another reminder that if you are not positively with Jesus then you will inevitably end up being against him.

>Jesus was often very harsh on the Pharisees, perhaps because they were the ones who knew the scriptures inside and out, and should have been the first to recognise all the prophecies about the Messiah being fulfilled in him. But it was probably because they thought they knew it all, that they could not accept it when it really happened. They had created a picture of the Messiah that they wanted, and Jesus just didn't fit the frame.

>But this can be true for us as well. It has often been said that man makes God in his own image.

It's easy to see this by looking at pictures of Jesus that have been drawn at different times by different cultures. For some people it's comforting to think of God as an old man in the sky who looks after them; they choose to forget that he is actually the Creator of the universe who will one day judge them.

Re-engage

The challenge is, to look at Jesus and really see him for who he is, not just what we would like him to be. The people of Ninevah, and the Queen of Sheba, as shown in the passage, responded to God without much evidence to persuade them. We're fortunate enough to have some pretty big clues to help us out – the record of Jesus' life, death and resurrection in the Bible.

>Do you have any preconceived ideas about Jesus that are hindering your view of him? Write them down and then have a good look at your list. Check them out against the Gospel accounts of Jesus' life.

Airlock: Dedicated

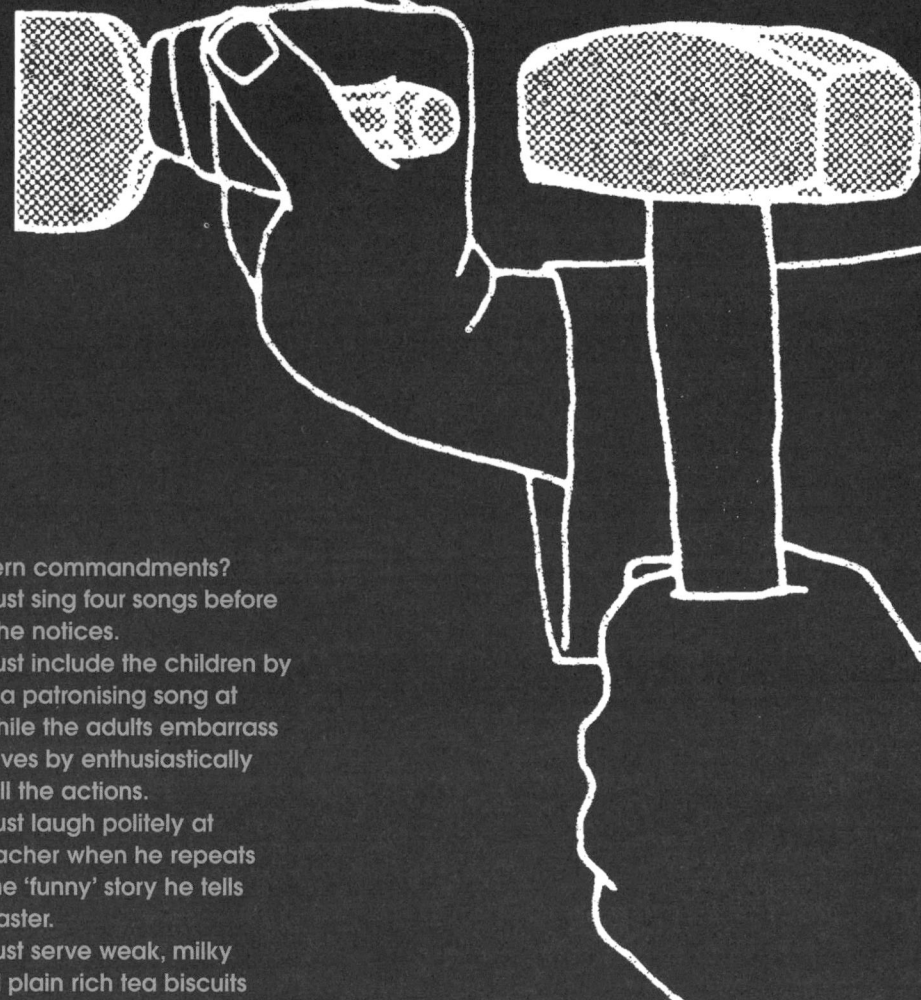

The modern commandments?
- Thou must sing four songs before giving the notices.
- Thou must include the children by singing a patronising song at them while the adults embarrass themselves by enthusiastically doing all the actions.
- Thou must laugh politely at the preacher when he repeats the same 'funny' story he tells every Easter.
- Thou must serve weak, milky tea and plain rich tea biscuits after the service.

What rules does your church have that are based more on tradition than on what the Bible says? How important is tradition anyway?

Extra_1 Romans 6:13–23
Extra_2 James 1:19–25

Live and let die

Decompress

What would you like to see written on your gravestone?

Now read Genesis 25:1–11

Immerse

Families today can be very complicated things. Some of us have parents who have divorced or are separated. Others have brothers or sisters who don't have the same biological parents as us. >Having different parents is nothing new, though. By the time he died, Abraham had had children by three different women – his first wife Sarah, his wife's servant Hagar, and his second wife Keturah. History shows us that their descendants did not get on well together, but Abraham had at least tried to make sure they were all provided for before he died.

Re-engage

How do you summarise 175 years? Abraham's life was full of incidents, adventures and experiences that few other humans have experienced, not even mentioning his conversations with God, yet the writer of Genesis summarises it as 'a long and satisfying life.' That's a summary I guess most of us would die for!

>There is not much any of us can do about the length of our life, except perhaps to live recklessly in a way that might shorten it! However, we can try to live a satisfying life. For Abraham, what was satisfying wasn't his wealth, or the number of children he had. It was the fact that he had heard and obeyed God's call. He had not always done what God had asked, but he put his faith in God, and 'that faith made him acceptable to God' (Genesis 15.6).

>What do you think God wants you to do with your life? Don't think career, ambitions or bank balance, although all these things are important. Draw a self portrait (don't worry, just draw a stick person if you're as graphically challenged as me!). Write around the picture of yourself the sort of character and person God wants you to be. Ask him to help you to be satisfied with seeking to achieve that, and to help you to achieve it.

Airlock: Dedicated

Very Important Person

D/12

Decompress

Have you ever felt 'second best' – that no matter what you do, you will never be as popular as someone else? Do you have scary memories about being the last one picked for a team? If so, you know how Ishmael must have felt.

Now read Genesis 25:12–18

Immerse

Ishmael honoured his father when he died: he joined Isaac in burying him. Abraham had made provision for him before he died. But there is always the feeling that he was not quite as important as Isaac. The writers of Israel's history are in no doubt about this – Ishmael's descendants are usually referred to as tribes that were a constant irritant to Israel. Isaac's descendants are the important ones – it is through his family tree that one day Jesus will emerge.

>Even though Abraham and the Israelites had favourites, God does not. He loved Ishmael as much as he loved Isaac. For him it is not a question of one being more important than the other, they were different but that does not imply relative importance.

>Sometimes we might feel second best – perhaps we're not as popular or significant as others in our family or our peer group. It is important to our self esteem that we feel valued by others. Well to the Supreme Being in the Universe, the Creator of everything, you are as important as prime ministers, presidents and the most popular person in your school or college.

>If you are one of the popular ones, bear in mind that to God you are no more significant than anyone else, and that he calls us to have the same attitude to others. 'Do not think you are better than you are. You must decide what you really are by the amount of faith God has given you.' (Romans 12.3)

Re-engage

Jesus never worried about being popular – he was far more concerned with doing what his heavenly father wanted.

>Who is the most popular person in your school or college? Do you wish you were as popular as other people? Popularity can be superficial. Make a conscious decision to be an open and honest friend to all, not spending all your energy and effort on trying to be popular.

>Who is the least popular person? How do you think they feel? Make a conscious decision to be friendly to them.

Airlock: Dedicated

Family fortunes

D/13

Decompress

'I want, I need, I have the right to...'
'You want, you need, I give you the right to...'
Which better describes the way Jesus treated others?

Now read Genesis 25:19–34

Immerse

Some rivalries are almost legendary – Arsenal vs Spurs or Liverpool vs Everton, for example. The fans and the teams take this rivalry very seriously, going all out to win games against their adversaries.

>The firstborn son in Isaac's day was the one who would inherit the bulk of the family estate. They would be the one through whom the family name and prestige would be continued. This was both a privilege and a responsibility that Esau seems not to have understood. He sold part of his rights for a bowl of soup, just because he was hungry and couldn't wait for the next meal.

>What is your birthright? Not something you might inherit from your parents, but something that God gives his spiritual children? 'God will give you the blessing he promised, because you are his child' (Galatians 4:7). Do you understand and appreciate the significance of this? It doesn't mean that you are invincible now, or that you will be rich and successful in material terms. What it means is that you have a guaranteed inheritance – eternal life and being a part of God's Kingdom.

Re-engage

Eternal life does not begin when you die, it starts now. God wants his heirs to live like they are his heirs, by adopting his values and living to bless and encourage others. We are to bear the family likeness. Unlike Esau, we cannot sell this divine birthright, but God does want us to try to give it away! Even if we give it to others, we cannot lose it ourselves.

>What do you think it means to be one of God's heirs? What do you think God would like you to do differently? Ask him to give you his Spirit to help you to do that.

>Is there someone with whom you know God wants you to share your inheritance?

Airlock: Dedicated

Like father, like son

D/14

Decompress

What does success look like in your life? Exam results, income, number of friends, possessions…?

Now read Genesis 26:1–35

Immerse

Successful people seem to become more unpopular the more successful they become. Famous people and their families are held up to public ridicule and scrutiny for no reason except that they are successful. Is it because the success of these people makes others jealous, or perhaps because the success makes the critics more aware of their own shortcomings?

>Isaac had become successful, so much so that Abimelech, the local tribal king, asked him to leave the area. Isaac had done nothing wrong, there was no reason to suspect that he was planning to take over. His only crime was to be successful. (And perhaps telling a little lie along the way.)

>How do you view success? Is it something to which you aspire, or is it something that you despise? Christians seem to be quite good at encouraging people to try their best in all things – working as if it was for Jesus – but if someone's work leads to material blessing, it is as if they have sold their soul to the devil.

Re-engage

There's nothing wrong with being successful or with possessions and money. These things only become wrong if they become obsessions and the focus of the attention and adoration that belongs to God – then we are guilty of idolatry as much as anyone in the Old Testament who bowed to a stone god. We can apply the same principle to people we love. They can become more important to us than God. That is a tricky balance to keep because we can see the people we love, but we can't see God so easily.

>Make a list of everything you would like to have. What lengths would you go to in order to get them? Would you lie, cheat, steal?

>Make a list of the people you love. Would you be willing to die to protect them? Do you love them more than you love Jesus?

>Ask God to help you to have his priorities for the things you have, the things you want, and the people you love. Ask him to help you to seek his Kingdom values first and not to worry about anything else.

Airlock: Dedicated

'Why you little…!'

D/15

Decompress

'An eye for an eye and a tooth for a tooth' – that way the whole world would be blind and toothless.

>'But I tell you, don't stand up against an evil person. If someone slaps you on the right cheek, turn to him the other cheek as well' (Matthew 5:39).

Now read Genesis 26:1–35

Immerse

Abimelech and his aides had not come to see Isaac to tell him to move on again. They were seeking a truce with him. After being moved on from place to place, even when he had been where God had told him, Isaac's home was now being established. Isaac's duplicity had become less significant to Abimelech when he saw how graciously Isaac moved on when others asked or forced him to go. He could see, too, that God was blessing him.

>Even though we might say or do things that let God down and perhaps make others think we are hypocrites, he doesn't want us to give up and stop trying to serve and honour him. If we are facing bullying or opposition we need to bear in mind that people take note of the way we respond. If we get aggressive or defensive they will not see any difference. However, if we 'turn the other cheek' or 'go the extra mile' we will be living Jesus' kingdom values and our reaction will be noticed.

>In *The Simpsons*, when Homer is the victim of Bart's mischief he usually responds by strangling Bart accompanied by the words "Why you little…" In the heat of the moment, we may be tempted to respond to people in the same way. Isaac had clearly got to the stage in his relationship with God that he was living much more by Jesus' Sermon on the Mount standards than the Old Testament standards of those around him.

Re-engage

Who really winds you up? Who is always niggling, annoying or even bullying you? How do you respond to them? Ask God to show you how you can respond in his way.

>What other circumstances might there be that are causing these people to act the way they are? What could you do to help?

Airlock: Dedicated

Many people misquote 'An eye for an eye and a tooth for a tooth', assuming that this is how we should respond when we are attacked. In fact, this was not setting the standard for retaliation, but the maximum allowed penalty.

Jesus' response in Matthew 5:39 seems to be extreme if we accept the interpretation of these words as being the way in which we should respond to attacks. But if an eye for an eye means that the most we should respond is with a proportionate response, it is not unreasonable for Jesus to show the opposite end of the scale – the way in which we could respond to show kingdom values.

Extra_1 Isaiah 50:4–9
Extra_2 Romans 12:17–21

History maker?

D/16

Decompress

How important is your history to you? How far back would you go to stake out who you are? A few years? To the year you were born? To your family history? To the history of your country?

Now read Acts 7:1–8

Immerse

We probably don't spend a whole lot of time looking back at history. We learn some stuff from it about politics and wars, but the future's where it's at. If you want something good and solid and exciting, come up with a new invention that will change the world.

>Which is all the total opposite of 2,000 years ago. Then, the future was unknown, scary and unproved. If you wanted something solid and exciting, you had to look back and find good solid roots in history. Which is why Jesus was scary. At this point in Acts, nobody had heard of Christianity. Followers of Jesus were a group of Jews who believed they'd found 'the Messiah'. But the way this 'Messiah' talked didn't seem to fit with their history for a lot of people. And if Jesus didn't fit with history, he must be wrong, because God doesn't change (they thought).

>If they wanted history, Stephen could give them history.

Re-engage

Stephen was set up as someone who disrespected the past and was following some new, unsound, untried, untested invention. But instead of cutting himself free from history, Stephen went right back to that history (and went a couple of stages further back than the people who set him up), to show how Jesus fitted in exactly with that history.

>So how does your history all fit together? Where was God first involved? Might he have been involved way before you even knew he existed? How does your history with God make a difference to the way you live your life now?

>Are there bits of your history you still don't get? Ask God to help you make enough sense of it to get on with now, and move on with him.

>If you've never done it before, write down your history with God, or draw a map of how you got this far. If you've done it before, find another Christian, ask them about how they got to where they are now, and be ready to tell them about your trip.

Airlock: Dedicated

The waiting game

Decompress

Has God ever made promises to you? What were they? Have they come true yet? If you're still waiting on any of them, how do you feel about that?

Now read Acts 7:9–18

Immerse

I'm not great at waiting. Never have been. I know that sometimes it's good to wait – presents at Christmas, sex and marriage, properly-cooked chicken, getting the proper training for a job. And when I look back, I'm glad I did wait – presents at Christmas. sex and marriage, properly-cooked chicken, getting the proper training for a job. Because not waiting can make the finished product a let down, cheap, dangerous or stressful. But it doesn't make waiting any easier.

>God seems to think waiting is a good idea. Before Jesus, his BIG plan took hundreds of years to come off, and at just about every stage that made up the BIG plan, people had to wait, and sometimes the waiting was as important as the 'getting there'.

Re-engage

Why was Stephen talking about Joseph when he was being stitched up for following Jesus? Maybe because he was pointing out that the people in charge – who were putting him on 'trial' – were looking at their history with the wrong contact lenses in. They might have looked at themselves and felt like kings – God's chosen people in their own land (apart from a few Roman governors), totally understanding everything about God and what he might do – but if they'd wound the clock back 1,850 years, they might have realised that God works in ways they really couldn't figure sometimes (God's promise seemed further away after Joseph, not closer). Maybe the people stitching up Stephen hadn't got their history – or God – as sorted as they thought?

>If God could work in ways they couldn't figure in 1850(ish) BC with Joseph, he could work in ways they couldn't understand in AD 30(ish) with Jesus (and Stephen), and in AD 2005(ish) with us.

>Spend some time in prayer asking God what his plan for you is. Make it a specific prayer request, but don't just look for his response in the quiet time after the prayer. Look into the Bible, listen to your Christian friends and see what God is doing in your life.

Airlock: Dedicated

Mistaken Identity?

Decompress

Stop. Breathe. Cut out the noise round you. Chill. And ask God to open your eyes to help you see him in any new ways you need to today.

Now read Acts 7:19–43

Immerse

God doesn't change, and most of us take him for granted as long as he keeps on producing the goods. The way we see him, what we understand about him, and the way we talk about him might change, but it's still the same God behind it all. It's a bit of a shame that the people Stephen was talking to just didn't seem to get that.

>What's Stephen's point with Moses? Here might be a few clues…

>Verse 25 – 'Moses thought his own people would understand that God was using him to save them, but they did not'…

>Verses 27 and 28 – 'Who made you ruler and judge? Are you going to kill me as you killed the Egyptian yesterday?'…

>Verse 35 – 'This Moses was the same man the two men of Israel rejected… the same man God sent to be a ruler and saviour… '

Verse 40 – 'But our ancestors did not want to obey Moses. They rejected him and wanted to go back to Egypt…' ..

>Moses is one of the biggest Old Testament guys. One of the most famous people ever to do stuff for God. But for a huge part of his life, nobody believed him. Loads of people missed who Moses was at the time, but it didn't change the fact that Moses was leading God's action. 1,850 years later, and loads of people were missing who Jesus was, but it didn't change the fact that Jesus was God in action…

>Are we open enough to God to hear when he's in action now? Whose side would we have been on here – Stephen the guy breaking the boundaries by following Jesus, or the leaders who were playing safe and sticking with what they knew?

Re-engage

Find someone who's been a Christian longer than you, and ask them if they've ever been in a situation where people couldn't agree if God was behind something or not. How did they make up their minds?

Airlock: Dedicated

Elvis has left the building

Decompress

If you can, get yourself somewhere that you find it easy to meet with God. Now.

Now read Acts 7:44–50

Immerse

The Temple was big news. There was only one Temple (even if it had been rebuilt a few times), the biggest and most amazing building they could build. And it was in Jerusalem. It was an important place, because it was a symbol of God meeting his creation. Right in the middle of it was the Most Holy Place, a place where one person would go just once a year to meet God. They had to tie a rope around him, so they could pull him out if he died in there. That's how big a deal it was.

>None of the people listening to Stephen would have seriously said that God actually lived in the Temple. Logically, they would have known that God isn't nailed down to any one place. And they'd have known that if God did just dwell in one place, he wouldn't be big enough or powerful enough to be worth following. But there is a very thin line between finding something or somewhere useful in finding God, and starting to live like that's the only way or place to find him or connect with him.

>The Temple had started out as a useful place for people to meet, and something to help people focus their eyes on God, but it was too easy for the Temple to be so much in the midst of looking for God, that it nearly became like a god. The Temple almost stopped being a useful symbol of God meeting people, and turned into a massive box which people could tie God down into and avoid for the rest of their 'real' lives.

Re-engage

Is there any danger that the places, people or ways you find help you to connect with God (maybe even the place you are now) become more of a focus than God himself. Is there a danger that you're stuffing God into a box and not letting him be himself?

>Find a Christian who connects with God in a totally different way to you, and meet God with them. You might find it easy. You might find it hard. But it might help God break out of the box which all of us find it too easy to stuff him into.

Busted

Decompress

When was the last time you felt like you'd been walked over? Think back to how you felt (or still feel). Are you OK with the way you handled the situation?

Now read Acts 7:51–60

Immerse

We're big on rights. Human rights. Worker's rights. Animal rights. Prisoner's rights. And, hey, we should be. God told us. "Make sure that orphans and foreigners are treated fairly…" (Deuteronomy 24:17 CEV). But Stephen seems to make a choice that the truth about God is more important than his own personal rights…

>The religious leaders hadn't liked what they'd heard from Stephen. All the way through his 'defence' he had been looking at the main players in the Old Testament from a new angle. And now he ends with telling them, the religious elite, that they're stubborn, don't listen to God, and work against the Holy Spirit. Everything their job description said they shouldn't be.

Re-engage

When I stop and look at Stephen, I can't believe his courage. He was the first person to die for being a Christian. Those first followers of Jesus had been given enough hassle to know their lives were on the line. But Stephen stuck with the truth, even if it was going to cost. And he didn't stand there yelling at people. He answered the leaders questions, and focused on Jesus. Even as he died, he was praying for the people chucking the stones (how like Jesus does that sound?). I think I'd have been picking the stones up and chucking them back. Maybe I'd have backed down before it even got that far, said sorry, done my best to forget about Jesus, and slipped off into a quiet corner of Jerusalem. We probably don't have to face risks like this (even if Christians do in other parts of the world), but we might need to learn from Stephen (who'd learnt from Jesus) about letting God live in us, even when we're misunderstood, disrespected or framed.

>Someone told me that more people have died in the last 100 years for being Christians than in all the 1,900 years before added together. Check out some websites (like www.opendoors.org). See what you can do to help Christians who risk their jobs, homes or even their lives by following Jesus today.

Airlock: Dedicated

>Some people think they can only pray if it they use thee and thou.
>Some people think they can only pray if they're jumping around in a crowd yelling.
>Some people think they can only worship God on a mountain.
>Some people think they can only worship God in a building with a spire that's been there longer than 300 years.
>Some people think they can only worship God if they're singing a song that was born after them.
>Some people think they can only worship God if they're singing a hymn that was born before their grandparents.
>Some people think they can only worship God if they're singing.
>Some people think they can only hear God in the King James Version of the Bible.
>Some people think they can only hear God from a preacher who's over sixty.
>Some people think they can only hear God from a preacher who's under thirty.
>Some people think only they can hear God.

Have we stuffed God in a box?

Extra_1 Genesis 1
Extra_2 Job 40,41

WAR! What is it good for?

Decompress

Today's reading is a song of praise. The Israelites have been saved (and will be saved again – BIG TIME), and they're well happy about it. Before you start, is there anything you want to praise God for?

Now read Isaiah 12

Immerse

This following chapters contain some serious action – death, destruction and devastation. This chapter is like a preparation for what we're about to read. It's like saying grace before you devour your food. Now, I have to be honest and say that I've read much more of the New Testament than I have of the Old Testament. The NT makes sense; it's about Jesus, and there aren't loads of bloody massacres.

>The OT does my head in sometimes, because there are so many wars, and most of them seem to be directed by God. But the Israelites were God's chosen people and he promised to always look after them. For years, they'd been enslaved by the Babylonians and now the time had come for Babylon to get some serious payback. I know there are loads of dictators I'd love to see blown off the face of the earth, and that's how the Israelites felt about Babylon.

Re-engage

It's hard to know what practical implication this has for our lives, isn't it? Chances are that none of us are going to have to go off into battle so what does this mean for us today? Well, the one thing that I've taken from this is that prayer and praise are the best forms of preparation. The Israelites are about to commence the mother of all battles with their former occupiers. You don't see them sharpening their swords or doing press-ups to prepare them for war. They're praying and praising, and if they can do that before going out to fight, then it's something we should do before we go out into the world.

>Think of a situation that you are currently involved in. As soon as you have identified it, spend some time praising God and praying to him. Try and put this into practice whenever you face a difficult situation.

>PS Remember that you can also praise and pray when things are OK! You're not a bad Christian if your life is going well!

Airlock: Dedicated

Let battle commence!

Decompress

What are your feelings about war? Do you think there are times when it is justifiable to go to war, or is it always wrong?

Now read Isaiah 13

Immerse

In this chapter of Isaiah, the attack on Babylon is for two reasons – firstly to free God's people from their slavery, and secondly to punish the Babylonians for straying from God.

>The language in this passage is pretty graphic – children getting beaten to death and women being raped (v 16). This isn't really what you'd expect from a loving and just God. I find it hard to take in, to be honest. How could God let that be done, and even worse, be done in his name, and even worse than that, be done as part of his plan? But before Jesus died for us, sin was a really big issue (it's still a big issue now, but you know what I mean). Before the crucifixion, people got punished directly by God. Now you (and I) might say 'well that's understandable, but rape is horrible, and hurting kids is awful!' But these people were being punished because they belonged to a sinning nation. Sin doesn't know any boundaries. And if Babylon was attacked for its sin, then everyone will suffer. Tough? Yes, but that's the way it was in those days.

Re-engage

What's the moral of all this? That's what I've been trying to work out. One thing that springs to mind is TAKE GOD SERIOUSLY. The Babylonians didn't, and look what happened to them. I've said it before, but I've always preferred the New Testament picture of a loving, gentle and kind God in the form of Jesus. He did get angry and he did have some incredibly challenging stuff to say. The God of the Old Testament is the same God, but he does show some different aspects. Anger, punishment, might and power. That's something I don't often think about, because maybe I've got too matey with him. Maybe we need to start taking what he says a bit more seriously.

>Are there any issues in your life that you aren't taking seriously? Is there any 'sin' that you aren't dealing with? The gift of Jesus is one of forgiveness. Use it, but take it seriously. Spend some time in prayer, dealing with the issues that you have.

I told you so

Decompress

More difficult questions today. Find a quiet spot on your own and ask God to help you understand what you're about to read.

Now read Isaiah 14:1–23

Immerse

I'm a big football fan and I love it when we're winning and we can sing and chant at the losing team and their supporters. And I guess that's pretty much how the Israelites felt. These verses are a great song, both of victory over the King of Babylon, and of praise to God for doing exactly what he said he would.

>Verse 9 reminds me of *Lord of the Rings - The Two Towers*, where the Ents get all mad because they see all the trees that Saruman has cut down. Isaiah often personifies nature, and it's really cool to think that everyone is so joyful that all the trees join in. The cedars of Lebanon were really special trees that had been chopped down and shipped away by Israel's oppressors for hundreds of years. It's like the Amazon rainforests rejoicing because they won't be destroyed anymore.

Re-engage

I like the idea of verses 18–20. In biblical days, a person's burial said a lot about them. It was important for a normal person to have a decent one, and a king's burial would be very impressive. So for the King of Babylon to have no grave, no burial, and to lie rotting with soldiers on the battlefield is a very bad way to go. No less than he deserved, I guess.

>It's important to remember that all of this is contained in a song of praise to God. And it was God that decided it was time for Babylon to get what was coming. Although there are maybe millions of people around the world, Christians included, who are ruled by evil leaders, it was God's perfect plan that brought Babylon to its knees. There are plenty of examples in the OT of God's people going into battle without him, and ending up in a right mess. We need to remember he has a perfect plan.

>Have a look at Jeremiah 29:11. How does this verse affect you? Spend some time in prayer talking to God about it..

Airlock: Dedicated

Trust in me!

Decompress

When was the last time you promised someone you'd do something, or the other way round? God is big on promises. When he says he'll do something, he does it. Before you start today, thank him for keeping his promises to you.

Now read Isaiah 14:24–27

Immerse

God's promises – in this case about war – DO go to plan. Verse 27 says 'When the All-Powerful makes a plan, no one can stop it'. How good is that?

>This is the God who we believe in. I have to say from personal experience, that life is SO good when you trust God. My future has seemed very uncertain recently – at work, at home and in my relationships. But I have been trusting totally in God to do what he has promised (to never leave me or forsake me (Joshua 1:5), to give me a safe future (Jeremiah 29:11)) and my faith has paid off.

Re-engage

In one of the young people's groups that I help run at our church, we do this thing called 'Good Week/Bad Week' where we say one positive thing and one negative thing that's happened since we last met. Now I'm not saying that when we trust in God nothing ever goes wrong, but the last few months there really have been very few bad things for me to say. And when there are, they're usually answered by the following week. So...

>For the next month, keep your own list of 'Good Week/Bad Week'. Thank God for the good stuff and pray that he'll help you to get through the bad things. Look back at times when he's answered your prayers, kept his promises, done things exactly according to his plan. Each day, tell him that your day is his and that you put everything in his hands. Trust me, or rather, trust him – it works. Then at the end of the month look back over the things you were worrying about and see how God dealt with them.

>If you discuss these questions as part of a regular group, try doing 'Good Week/Bad Week' together.

>If God hasn't answered your prayers about something, why do you think that is?

They think it's all over...

D/25

Decompress

I'm a big football fan, and I've been to a lot of matches where it looks like it's all over, but then there's a twist at the end – a surprise goal, a last minute penalty, a 90th minute punch-up. As Christians we need to always be prepared for what will happen next.

Now read Isaiah 14:28–32

Immerse

If you want to do some historical digging, it's thought that these verses refer to a revolt by the Philistines against Sargon of Assyria. Go and do a search on the net for him and see what you come up with.

>1 Peter 1:13 says 'So prepare your minds for service and have self-control. All your hope should be for the gift of grace that will be yours when Jesus Christ is shown to you.' I'm starting to get into the practice of trying to 'prepare my mind' every day. I pray that God will be with me in my decisions, help me to follow his way, and protect me from anything that may harm me.

Re-engage

We don't want to be bitten by the dangerous, poisonous snakes that exist in our world today. Once we've overcome a problem, there may be another that crops up straightaway in its place. It's only with God's help that we can overcome sustained spiritual attack from the devil. Pray to God each day and prepare your mind.

>Has there been a period in your life when you've felt under constant attack? What was it like? How did you deal with it? Think about how Jesus dealt with constant attacks a) during his time of temptation in the desert and b) from the leaders and teachers of the law during his time of ministry.

>I'm a firm believer in spiritual warfare. As Christians, we are always under attack. Even if it doesn't feel like it, we are. And sometimes it feels like just when we think the hard times are all over – something else comes up and hits us in the guts. We need to be prepared for Satan's attacks. They often come when we least expect them.

How can we enjoy victory –
in anything from sport to war –
while still acting in a Christian way?

Extra_1 Psalm 60
Extra_2 Luke 14:7–11

Adopted in your family

Decompress

'Lord, help me to do your will and be a part of the family of heaven. Amen.'

Now read Matthew 12:46–50

Immerse

No, Jesus hasn't hit his head. He's not suddenly developed amnesia and forgotten who his real mother and brothers are. It's what is commonly known as 'making a point'. Here, Jesus defines his true family as anyone who does what his father in heaven wants, so much so that he leaves his real family (Mary and his brothers) outside on the doorstep, struggling to get in to give him a message.

>Just a few short chapters ago, Jesus told his followers that their relationships with their families should be less important that their relationship with him (Matthew 10:35–38). Now he's putting it into effect with a practical demonstration, showing that his followers are the true members of God's family because they follow his teaching.

>That sounds a bit harsh on his real family, doesn't it? But Jesus wasn't disowning his real family, or saying that they weren't his followers (because they were –

check out who stays with him to the bitter end in John 19:25). He's saying that anyone and everyone can be part of his true family – by listening to Jesus and obeying God. And that doesn't just mean people who lived 2,000 years ago, it means you and me. Which is good news, if you ask me.

Re-engage

Make a list of your family members, including those people who you see as being in your 'spiritual' family. Now make a commitment to pray for those people every day this week.

>Are you part of Jesus' family? Do you do everything that your father in heaven wants? Not easy is it? What do you struggle with most? Don't be discouraged! Even those people that Jesus refers to in this passage as being his true family (ie his disciples) messed up at times. Keep on going, trusting that God is with you!

Airlock: Dedicated

Birdseed?

Decompress

'Lord, help me to hear the message of your kingdom, and to grow and produce fruit.'

Now read Matthew 13:1–17

Immerse

Jesus says something very strange in verse 11. He says that the kingdom of God is a secret and that some people aren't allowed to know it. That seems very confusing. Surely the gospel message is for everyone?

>Well, yes it is. Jesus isn't saying that some people aren't allowed to hear the good news, he's referring back to the parable. Some people will hear the good news, and choose not to listen. They're like the seed that falls by the roadside (for more explanations, see D/28). Everyone hears the message but the ones that choose not to listen are not allowed to hear the secrets about the kingdom of heaven.

Re-engage

This is one of Jesus' most famous parables, but I'd never actually read it properly until now. I always assumed that he talked about seeds, the people looked puzzled, and he said 'Well, here's what I really mean...' But he doesn't do that. He tells everyone the parable, doesn't explain it, and ends with a cryptic 'You people who can hear me, listen!' so that people go off in a confused fashion.

>Maybe he didn't want easy explanations. Maybe he wanted them to go away and talk about what he'd said, to argue about it. Maybe he wanted the crowds to do some of the work themselves, to think about what he meant, to puzzle over why a farmer would waste so much seed.

>Maybe he means the same for us too. The Bible is by no means an easy book to get to grips with, and there are bits that need thinking about, need arguing about, need discussion. And it's not just a command for us to talk about the Bible with each other – we've got to respond positively as well.

>Which bits of the Bible do you find difficult to understand? Are there whole books that you avoid? Why not try reading a commentary on difficult passages? Or have a 'difficult Bible passages' night at your youth group and talking through the ones that really make you scratch your head. Invite your vicar (or someone else in the know) along to help you understand them (although it might be best to warn them beforehand so they can come prepared).

Airlock: Dedicated

I'm sorry, I haven't a clue

D/28

Decompress

'Lord, help me to understand your word when I find it difficult, and help me to relate it to my life and the way you want me to live. Amen.'

Now read Matthew 13:18–23

Immerse

There's nothing I like more than getting swept up in the plot of a can't-put-it-down book. I'll sit and read for a whole weekend if the story is gripping enough. Good stories have a way of pulling you in, of demanding your attention, of making you think and dream and turn the page to find out what happens next.

>Jesus loved telling stories. He recognised that people really engage with a story well told, and that he could teach them really massive and complex truths with very simple stories. He related things back to their own life with stories about things like farming, cooking and travelling, and made it exciting. He even used cliffhangers – this passage is the explanation to the parable found in Matthew 13:1–17.

>Jesus talks about four different ways of responding to the gospel. The seed (the gospel) stays the same in all the instances, but the soil it is sown into (the individual) changes, depending on how receptive people are to the message (v 20), or how much they are affected by other things (the devil, v 19; the world, v 22).

Re-engage

It's interesting to note that the seed that bears fruit isn't representative of the person who only hears Jesus' message – it's representative of the person who hears the message and also understands it. And with understanding comes some kind of call to action. You can't just go to church every Sunday and sit back saying 'my job here is done'. It's not just about learning, it's about learning, understanding and doing.

>Jesus told stories because they were culturally relevant. Think about some different ways we could retell the Gospel message today that would hold people's attention. How about a website? Some graffiti? A musical? A board game? Why not do it!

Airlock: Dedicated

Virtue or impossibility

D/29

Decompress

'Lord, help me to have patience when faced with difficult situations, and give me the knowledge that you are with me at all times. Amen.'

Now read Matthew 13:24–30,36–43

Immerse

Patience is a virtue apparently. But sometimes it feels like an impossibility. Like opening Christmas presents before Christmas Day or downloading an album before it's been released in the shops – having to wait for something to happen can be maddening and frustrating and even disillusioning.

> Jesus' divine nature must have been pretty confusing to his followers. They lived in a culture that expected the Messiah to come back and immediately make things better – to get rid of the Roman occupation and to rid the world of oppression and injustice overnight. But Jesus was doing things in a different way. He'd started off by talking to fishermen, by telling stories to the common people. And here he goes further and tells the disciples that things are going to be the way they are until the day of judgement. The

people, who were hoping to see God come again in power and wipe out poverty and suffering, were going to have to be patient for a bit longer.

Re-engage

Let's be honest – it can be really hard being patient with God. We expect him to carry out things according to our time scale. I'm in the middle of a situation right now that I've been praying about for ages, and as of yet I haven't had an answer. It's been really hard to still have faith that my prayers will be answered.

> Do you keep a prayer diary? It can help to see how God has answered prayer in the past, and be a real encouragement for the future. Why not start one, listing all the things you thank God for, and that you ask God for. Go back at the end of every month and see how your prayers have been answered and be encouraged.

> What are you praying for at the moment that God doesn't seem to be answering? Should we ever give up on a prayer if God doesn't answer it straight away, or should we be persistent?

Airlock: Dedicated

Small is beautiful?

D/30

Decompress

'Lord, help my faith to grow and to bear fruit. Amen.'

Now read Matthew 13:31–35

Immerse

Little things grow big. An acorn grows into an oak tree. A stream becomes a river becomes an ocean. A small border conflict erupts into full blown civil war. A baby grows into an adult. Alice eats a little cake on her way to Wonderland and grows enormous.

>Little things grow big. A tiny bit of faith can grow into something enormous.

>The mustard seed is a tiny seed that grows into a bush big enough for birds to nest in its branches. It only takes a tiny bit of yeast to effect a lot of bread.

>Jesus says in this passage that the kingdom of heaven is like that – it's started off small and insignificant almost, with Jesus standing at the water's edge and calling a few fishermen to follow him, and yet it's going to grow into something enormous that will impact the lives of millions of people and ultimately affect the whole world.

Re-engage

It's all very well saying that faith can grow from something small to something enormous, but how does it happen? It's by no means an easy thing to do, but the simple answer is to keep trusting God in everything you do – through the good times and (especially) the bad times, through the happy times and (especially) the sad. If you let God lead and guide you through whatever life throws at you, your faith will grow.

>I know it's difficult. When you're going through a really rough time, it's very hard to trust that God's got things under control and that he's got a plan for your life. But eventually you come out the other end and it's like the clouds parting and the sun being revealed. You can look back and see that God has been there all along, and he has got good things in store for us.

>If you are going through a rough time, hang on in there. Keep reading your Bible. Keep talking to your close friends about it. Keep talking to God. Things will improve. Have faith.

Airlock: Dedicated

Go and buy a packet of mustard
seeds. They're dead cheap, and
you can get them from garden
centres and the like. First of all,
open the packet and get one out.
Tiny isn't it?

Now find a plant pot (also available
in garden centres, cheap DIY
shops, and from your dad's garden
shed) and plant the mustard seed,
following the instructions on the
back of the packet. Look after it
and water it. Watch as the tiny seed
grows and grows (if you're looking
after it right).

See that mustard seed? The one
that used to be tiny and is now
massive? That's the kingdom of
heaven in your life, that is.
How cool is that?

Extra_1 Mark 4:30–34
Extra_2 Luke 17:5,6

The King and I

D/31

Decompress

'So always be ready, because you don't know the days your Lord will come' Matthew 24:42.

Now read Psalm 24

Immerse

When you ask the question 'Can I ascend the hill of the Lord?' you don't really expect the answer 'Only if your hands are clean' and you've a willingness to 'try and follow God.' I love that phrase – it gives hope to all those of us who frequently stumble up the hill trying to do our best and end up face down in a puddle with mud on our faces!

>In our house, we were always taught to wash our hands after we'd visited the toilet and also before we ate, to get rid of the germs we picked up during the day. As Christians, there are two ways we can get dirty hands – by our whopping great obvious deliberate sins, but also from the irritating everyday sins that somehow get stuck to us. God knows it's hard, and that's why he provided Jesus and his water of life...

>It gets hard when we talk about big sins and little sins – they're all the same size to God. But we naturally hone in on the sins we decide are 'big' and sometimes ignore the everyday ones, which often cause more trouble for the people around us. Can you identify any everyday sins that need to be washed away?

Re-engage

Who is this glorious King? Perhaps that's the biggest question for us as Jesus' disciples. It's all very well doing that 'shout out words of praise about God' thing they do in trendy churches, but sometimes it's difficult to build up a picture of another person just from other people's experiences of them. We need to draw on our own experiences of Jesus – through our own lives as well as through the Bible and prayer.

>Spend ten or fifteen minutes thinking about the places that you have met Jesus or seen him in someone else, and use this to help you to start thinking about who the Lord all-powerful really is...

Airlock: Dedicated

The praise of the broken

D/32

Decompress

'The time is coming when the true worshippers will worship the Father in spirit and truth, and that time is here already. You see, the Father too is actively seeking such people to worship him' John 4:23.

Now read Psalm 25

Immerse

I love this psalm. It's one of the most cringe-free praise songs I've ever come across – and there's not an action in sight!

>The modern worship song 'No one whose hope is in you' is based around the first seven verses of the psalm, but take a look at verses 16-20. You wouldn't catch a congregation singing those in church! This psalm wasn't written by David on a happy clappy day, but in broken and desperate times. And that is what gives the psalm its strength and passion. So highlight your Bible, memorise the verses and keep it for a lousy day. Because while our hope is in the Lord, we may be broken, but he will never let us be put to shame.

>'The Lord is good and right; he points sinners to the right way' (v 8). Definitely something to be grateful for! The glorious King is prepared to associate himself with sinners, with the likes of you and me. But there are two attitudes he needs from us to be able to teach us – humility (v 9) and respect (v 12).

Re-engage

There are some praise songs used in church which, quite frankly, I find embarrassing. I'm not really embarrassed because they're blasphemous, or even because they've got a cheesy tune. It's just that some of the words appear to have been written for Christian robots rather than the standard, everyday, emotionally-rollercoastering human being, and I can't cope with singing about waving flags and stamping on people when I'm not in the mood.

>But there have also been praise songs written that allow me to communicate with God no matter what sort of mood I'm in. The sort of songs where the truth is so clear that it's impossible not to worship in spirit and truth. This is one example of such a song of praise. So why not use it – make up your own tune, feel free to wander off into your own words and worship in spirit and truth!

Airlock: Dedicated

Guilty by association?

D/33

Decompress

Jesus answered … "It is not the healthy people who need a doctor, but the sick. I have not come to invite good people but sinners to change their hearts and lives"' Luke 5:30–32.

Now read Psalm 26

Immerse

'Lord, I love being at church where you live, where your glory is.' How often do we proclaim this? How often do we think of our church being the residence of God, and the place where he shows his glory? And how often do we think of our church resembling a rowdy meeting where everyone simply has to get their point of view about various important issues such as the flower rota, choice of hymns and interior design across?

>Church is a very difficult issue for a lot of us, particularly as young people. Most churches are run by middle-aged people who have their own views on how church services should proceed, which coincidentally are usually the complete opposite of our own.

>Yet we seem to have forgotten that, rather than being the place where we come to worship, church is the place where God lives and his glory is seen. I know it's difficult and tiresome when you feel like you're stuck in a TV programme for which only four episodes have been made and they are being repeated over and over, but do you ever go to church expecting to see God's glory? If not, try talking to him next time you go over to his house…

Re-engage

Look at the first three verses of the Psalm. If you're brave enough, pray them. What issues and ideas does God bring to mind? Write them down and work out how to deal with them – discuss them with other Christians if you need to.

>Jesus, David, Paul, Samson, Abraham, Joseph, Esther… All very different people with very different attitudes to the non-Jewish people surrounding them. God delights in differences and always knows how to use them to his advantage. What are your strengths and weaknesses, and who is God calling you to minister to? Are there any people that you need to avoid hanging around with in order to build your strength up and stay innocent?

Airlock: Dedicated

The beautiful and the bold

D/34

Decompress

'I truly believe I will live to see the Lord's goodness. Wait for the Lord's help. Be strong and brave, and wait for the Lord's help' Psalm 27:13,14.

Now read Psalm 27

Immerse

It's such a pity that humans have turned into such pessimistic creatures, focused by the media on the trials, tribulations and other gruesome bits of life. As Christians, we should obviously not ignore the pain in the world. However, we should always have in our minds that God created this world to be perfect and just because his perfection has been distorted, it doesn't mean that it has vanished.

>There are so many images of God's perfection around, and if we keep these in mind whilst we are dealing with the pain, then I would suggest that we stand a much better chance of discovering God's beauty amongst these days of trouble.

Re-engage

What do you think of the phrase 'if my father and mother leave me, the Lord will take me in'? The Lord has been my light and salvation, he's been my protector and has even taken me in when I've been in trouble with my mum and dad. In order to do this, God has worked through many different people who have shown God's light, protection and love. And do you know, on a couple of occasions I've even felt God working through me to protect and guide some of my friends.

>The nature of the Psalms can feel very isolated – after all, they're conversations between a single person and God. But never be tricked into thinking that God is always working at some higher level that we have to leap to attain – he's communicating on your frequency!

>Where have you seen the beauty of God over the last week? Who are the people that God works through to encourage bravery and courage in you? Are you spending enough time with them?

>There's a very important message in verses 13 and 14. Do you believe it?

Airlock: Dedicated

God's filing cabinet

Decompress

'But I say to you, love your enemies. Pray for those who hurt you. If you do this, you will be children of your Father in heaven' Matthew 5:44,45.

Now read Psalm 28

Immerse

Isn't it strange how often David moans about his enemies in the Psalms? I mean, you don't find many vicars these days encouraging their congregations to join together in a time of sharing insults about their enemies…

> David's plea for God to repay his enemies by knocking them down does not sit comfortably with Jesus' teaching to love our enemies But you know what, our pathetic mumblings of prayers for our enemies do not impress Jesus either.

> There is no point in pretending to God that there are no such things as enemies, and that we are just one great big hunk of love in a big lovely world. How can we love our enemies if we don't understand why they're our enemies in the first place? Admitting what causes us to dislike our enemies is the first step towards this understanding, and who knows, perhaps we'll be able to pray for our differences rather than sweeping them under the

carpet. You never know, we might even go one step further and start forgiving them…

Re-engage

God answers prayers in his own time. This doesn't mean that he has a three class filing system marked 'prayers to be answered now', 'prayers to be answered later' and the waste paper bin for 'prayers to be thrown away'. Just because the answer doesn't always come immediately doesn't mean that he's got the answer-phone switched on and hasn't bothered to pick up his messages yet! No, God listens to our prayers straight away and sets to work on answering them in the most powerful and sensible way possible. He knows exactly when we need to hear from him, and exactly when we need to find something out for ourselves with just the gentlest of guidance. That's what makes him God, I suppose…

> When you next pray to God, have faith that he's listening and that he hears you. As soon as you've prayed, your prayer has been answered! You might not find out what the answer is yet, but have faith, because God is always working his purpose out for the best… go on… pray!

Airlock: Dedicated

Psalm 25 was written as an acrostic poem – with each line beginning with the letters of the Hebrew alphabet in order. So as well as writing a stunningly good praise song, David would also have been able to pass his GCSE Hebrew Language exam...

Write your own acrostic poem here (in English – although you could try writing it in Hebrew if you like!)

A

B

C

D

E

F

G

H

I

J

K

L

M

N

O

P

Q

R

S

T

U

V

W

X

Y

Z

Other acrostic psalms
Extra_1 Psalm 34
Extra_2 Psalm 37

Doing the right job

Decompress

'Father, help me to know what my gifts are and to use them well.'

Now read 1 Corinthians 12:1–11

Immerse

When I was in college, I was involved in student radio. I did a radio show for a while, and eventually, I got myself elected as president of the college radio station. Yay! I thought. I'm in charge! Except I hadn't the faintest idea what to do or how to do it. By the time I finished, it was a miracle the station was still running. I'd made a basic error – I assumed that because I could make a decent go of presenting a radio show (although, frankly, it wasn't that great) I was going to able to run the whole show. And I just wasn't. I had a place, I had a part to play… and it wasn't running the radio station.

>Paul was writing to the church in Corinth about how to get on. The people in the church had got involved in a series of arguments about all sorts of things – which teachers they were listening to, whether one of the people in the church should have taken another one to court … the list was, and is, depressing. Here, Paul's addressing the argument they had about spiritual gifts – some of the people in the church were doing some pretty spectacular things, and they were making out that this made them more important than their fellow believers.

Re-engage

The people Paul was talking to when he wrote this bit of the letter were able to do some pretty spectacular things – they could heal, they could prophesy the future, they spoke in different languages. But they wasted time arguing about which of them was the most important, and didn't achieve nearly as much as they could because of all the bickering.

>Christians today sometimes suffer from the same problem. We need to recognise that God gave us the same Holy Spirit, and we're all heading for the same reward. We shouldn't be conceited about what we can do, because it's a gift from God. And if we find that what we're doing is failing miserably, it just might be because it's not what we're gifted in.

>Think about the gifts you have. Are you using them? Is what you're doing the right thing for you? Think and pray about it. Be honest with yourself – you might be happier doing something completely different.

Airlock: Dedicated

The body matters

Decompress

Ever feel like you're not important? Or that you've got nothing to give?

Now read 1 Corinthians 12:12–26

Immerse

Imagine a football team with 11 strikers. No goalkeeper, no defenders, no midfielders, just 11 guys all right at the front of the field, going for the goal, all doing their best to score at any cost.

>They might be footballing legends. They could be the 11 greatest goal scorers the world has ever seen, but I guarantee you that they'd lose against any half-decent team. Why? Because they're not going to hold together. No one's going to feed them the ball. No one's going to be standing in the goal. They're all so busy trying to do the same thing, they fail to do all the other stuff which is also important. As a result, they won't succeed in doing anything at all.

>Any group of people with a common purpose needs people with different talents and skills – and it needs those people to survive and grow. Why is it that the Church tends to concentrate so much on some people and not on others?

>Those pesky Corinthians. They spent so much time bickering about who was the most important, they failed to achieve much at all. Paul's point is basically this: if you're a Christian, then Jesus has sent the Holy Spirit to live in you. It doesn't matter how the Spirit shows itself in you, you have a part to play just like everyone else.

Re-engage

It doesn't matter what you can do for God, there's an important and necessary place for you. Don't ever feel that you're not gifted in any useful way. On the other hand, if you find yourself up the front, leading, teaching or whatever, you shouldn't feel that you're better than any other Christian. We've all got our part to play, and we're all needed. God sees us all equally, and loves us all equally.

>What can you give? You might think you've got nothing to offer, but you'd be surprised. Everyone has something to give, and everything is necessary. It could be anything from hoovering the floor to writing letters to singing or playing in a band. Whatever it is, if you give it cheerfully, knowing that God's behind whatever you do for him, God will honour that. So what can you give? Go on, have a think!

Airlock: Dedicated

Up front

Decompress

'Father, help me to be open to whatever you've got in store for me.'

Now read 1 Corinthians 12:27–31

Immerse

Being the leader isn't always a desirable thing. Sure, you have authority over others, but you've also got responsibility for them, and if you get it wrong, you get the blame. You see it again and again, with managers of football teams, managing directors of big companies, and political leaders. The buck stops with them. They have to make the hard choices. They often have the hardest jobs.

>Paul has come to this bit of his letter to the Corinthians in the middle of telling them that they're all equal in God's sight, and that they shouldn't get conceited about their gifts. At this point, he concedes that while God looks at us all equally, ultimately God's going to give some people the gifts they need to lead the rest of us. There's been so much arguing about this among the Corinthians, that Paul feels he's got to quickly set out a chain of command.

Re-engage

The people who are put in positions of responsibility in the Church have been put there by God, and we've got to respect that, and, more importantly, respect them.

>The next set of gifts – the doing of miracles, speaking in different languages and interpreting them, healing and so on – are things we all have potential to do. In fact, Paul not only says that we might all be able to be gifted with these things by God, he actually encourages us to want to do them. Not everybody (or even that many people) are going to be doing these things, and if God's decided to make you the person to do this, you're going to have a great deal of responsibility to use the gift you've been given wisely and to always remember that it's a gift from God. You're not doing these things, God is – don't ever think you're superior to other Christians because he's chosen you to use a special gift.

>You should seriously – and honestly – consider whether you've got gifts in these areas. The Christian church needs more people to lead, more people to say the things that need to be said, more people who can pray and see things done, more people who can go out on the streets and tell people about Jesus. Are you cut out for this? Pray about it. Pray for the gifts to do this stuff.

Airlock: Dedicated

(Nearly) all need you need

Decompress

'Father, help me to be patient with the people around me; let love be the centre of all I say and do.'

Now read 1 Corinthians 13:1-13

Immerse

I know a woman who's one of the most solid Christians I know. She knows her Bible inside out, she's got piles of theological books, she plays in a worship group, she even writes songs. But none of it works for her. Her problem is this – she just doesn't like people. She's had a whole pile of bad experiences and she won't trust anyone anymore. She expects the worst of people and assumes that her opinions are the only true ones. She'll never let you forget it if you've wronged her, and she'll make sure that other people know. She is possibly the unhappiest and loneliest person I know.

>Up to this point, Paul's written a whole manual on how to run a church, what to do, what not to do, what to worry about, what to disregard, how to avoid arguments. This is the part where he's taking a deep breath and saying, 'Look. You're missing the whole point. This is the point...'

>It's born out of frustration with the Corinthians and what he's heard about them. They argue about who's the most important, who's the best spiritual leader to follow. They humiliate each other by trying to outdo each other at their church meals. The richer members of the church don't share their food with the poorer people. And they even take each other to court. Here's the part where Paul, almost at the end of his tether, tells the bickering, petty, selfish Corinthians how it can all be avoided.

Re-engage

Paul's point is about as simple as it gets – if you base it all around love, all the errors he's talked about in the rest of the letter can be avoided. All of them.

>And the way he puts it, it's pretty obvious it's an active thing. This passage gets read a lot as if it's a sweet and fluffy list of nice things. But it's really one of the angriest passages of scripture. It's a hard thing to do. You have to will yourself into loving the person next to you even if every instinct is screaming at you to smack them in the face. You have to will yourself into keeping quiet when that really fantastic put-down line pops into your head. You have to make yourself love, and it won't be easy. Fortunately, we've got God to give us a hand. He will, if we ask him.

Airlock: Dedicated

Speak

Decompress

'Lord, show me the gifts you want me to show, and help me to be able to speak out against the injustices I see with courage.'

Now read 1 Corinthians 14:1-5

Immerse

A friend of mine got a job a few years back in a customer service call-centre for a big phone company. She hated it. They had inflexible working hours, they treated their staff really badly, they wouldn't allow the trade union on the premises, they encouraged staff to tell on their colleagues for terrible crimes like emailing people. My friend, who is a Christian, spent her entire time there protesting about the things which were wrong, and she repeatedly got into trouble with the bosses. She lasted six months.

>When she left, to her surprise the staff threw a party for her. One of them said to her, 'I wish I had your faith. It comes out in everything you do.' It turned out that although she was widely hated by the bosses, she was widely admired and liked by the people on the shop floor, and gave a lot of them the courage to stand for some decent working practices.

>Many people think that the gift of prophecy just involves predicting the future, but it's a lot more than that. Most of the prophecies found in the Bible are less about predicting what's going to happen and more telling people what God thinks about the current order of things. Take Amos, Hosea, Micah, Jeremiah, Isaiah, and even John the Baptist. All of them told the people around them exactly what God thought about what the people of their day were doing, and it wasn't pretty.

Re-engage

Like my friend in the call centre, people with the gift of prophecy simply tell it like it is (and sometimes how it will be), regardless of the trouble it's going to get them into or the friends it's going to lose them. It's a hard path, being a prophet, as anyone who's been one will tell you. But if you do find yourself doing this, God will be behind you all the way. And you may even see results.

>Don't be afraid to speak out. Pray for God to guide what you have to say, and make a stand for the poor, the dispossessed, the downtrodden, the seekers of asylum. Find out about organisations that make a stand for these people – groups like Amnesty, Christian Solidarity Worldwide, the Jubilee Debt Campaign. See if there's anything you can do.

Airlock: Dedicated

Take the list of characteristics of
love as given in 1 Corinthians 13 –
patient, kind, does not brag, is not
proud etc – and write them down in
a list. Now replace the word 'love'
with your name. Look at the list.
How accurately does it describe
you? Now keep it – stick it on the
wall or something – and try and live
up to it. Pray that you can.

Extra_1 Song of Solomon 8:6,7
Extra_2 1 John 4:7–21

The big one from the Big One

Decompress

'Dear Lord, help me to understand the words that you spoke so many years ago through your prophet Zephaniah. Let them speak to me today in all I think, do and say.'

Now read Zephaniah 1:1–18

Immerse

To make a really big disaster movie you first need to set the scene. Whether it's the discovery of a comet the size of Bolton heading in the earth's direction or the disruption of satellite TV by giant spacecraft creating radio wave interference, the set up is all-important. The bigger the impending disaster, the bigger the threat, and the bigger the film, the bigger the resolution etc.

>The way this prophecy from Zephaniah gets under way, you'd think the special effects guys are going to be in for a really hard time. This is the big one, the end of the world and it's got nothing to do with aliens attacking the planet or big rocks hurtling towards the earth and threatening to wipe out all human life. This is the big one from the Big One – God's had enough, and he's going to do something about it.

Re-engage

Zephaniah gives a nice long list of reasons why God is going to enact some divine judgement, primarily concerned with the worship of other gods. It's very easy for us to put other things before God, and not give him his due respect, although I suppose most of us don't have a statue of Molech or Dagon in our bedroom.

>But verse 6 tells us that the people who God was going to punish didn't necessarily have to worship other gods in order to be destroyed – they just had to turn their backs on God. In his eyes, that's equally as catastrophic. And that's so relevant for us today. Turning our backs on God, whether it's for good or for a few minutes while we do something that we know he's not going to approve of, can have serious consequences!

>Spend some time praying that God will be there to guide you throughout this day; that his directions will be clear for you to see, and that he will give you the strength to carry out his will.

Airlock: Dedicated

Not CTRL-ALT-DELETE

Decompress

Take a moment to reflect on how you are doing at the moment. Where have you got to in your life? Are you confident in yourself? Where does your strength come from?

Now read Zephaniah 2:1–15

Immerse

If you know anything about computers you'll know how vital the CTRL + Z key combination is. It allows you to undo a mistake. Whilst you are working in a text or a graphics programme, if you make a mistake or realise you don't want the picture to look quite that way, then you can retrace your steps. A piece of writing or a picture can look quite different with a couple of taps on the undo keys.

>In chapter 1 of Zephaniah's prophecy, it looked like it was all doom and gloom. However, here we have the offer of an undo key, a way back to God.

>There is a lot about not being proud in this passage. God's people are warned not to be proud, but to humble themselves before God. Likewise, the other nations seem to be heading for a fall because of their pride.

Re-engage

Remember what was said in Zephaniah 1 about the whole world being destroyed, disaster is a-coming? It is refreshing to hear the words in these first few verses. God is giving the hearers of this message a CTRL + Z button to push.

>That is one of the best things about prophetic words from God – they are there to help us change our ways, to draw closer to him. Despite all his people had done, he was still offering them a way back. And despite all that we may have done, however dark or bad the deeds, these words are for us. All we need to do is lay down our pride...

>Do you need to hit the undo keys in an area of your life? Talk to God about it and humble yourself before him. He'd love to have a chat with you!

The choice reloaded

Decompress

'Dear Lord, let my speech be pure so that I may speak your name and worship you.'

Now read Zephaniah 3:1–13

Immerse

The Matrix Trilogy caused a lot of people a lot of headaches as they tried to work out what was going and what all the cod-philosophy was about, particularly when the Oracle showed up. The concepts of choice and freedom are key concepts in the films.

They're also key concepts to Christians. Now I don't intend to summarise the whole theology of predestination but what I do want to say is that we are, to an extent, victims of the circumstances that we find ourselves in. Our choices can be seen as being limited by the situations we live in. For example, if we are educated we can do... or if we are rich we can do... etc.

>In the same way, if we have met God, we can do... if we love God, we can/should do... etc.

>If God has been active in your life, how should you be living now?

Re-engage

The leaders of Jerusalem are given a bit of a going over here. It is good to compare the sins of the other nations with the sins of God's people. Morally, the other nations should have acted in different ways. God's people not only have the moral reason for not sinning but also God's revealed truth, and everything that God has done for them in the past (vs 6,7). But it hasn't made much difference to the way they live their lives.

>How do you live your life? Is your life lived in response to what God has done for you? Time and again, the Jewish people are called back to God by his prophets. What is God saying to you today, here and now?

>Start writing a list of things that God has done for you in your prayer journal, and update it regularly. When you notice that you are slipping away from him, take out the list and use it as a basis for worship to bring you closer to his presence.

Airlock: Dedicated

It's not the end of the world

D/44

Decompress

'Dear Lord, help me to draw close to your words in order to hear them, to understand them and to act on them.'

Now read Zephaniah 3:14–20

Immerse

Being a bit strange, many disaster movies fail to really excite me. The reason being that, in the end, and obviously to keep the cinema-going-public happy, the world gets saved. Recently a few films like *Armageddon* and *Deep Impact* have destroyed bits of it, although frequently they are not the bits that I would like to see flattened. On the whole, though the planet remains to fight another day.

>The end of Zephaniah appears to follow the true style of Hollywood disaster stories – in other words, it promises a happy ending. Boy, it was going to be bad but now (as seen in verse 14) it is going to be great.

>Despite all that we do, God keeps giving us more and more chances to come back to him. Reading through the Old Testament it may seem that God is a very angry God who goes around smiting and crushing all who stand in his way. However, the truth is different. Time and again, God warns his people to change their ways. He also shows the other nations how powerful he is by what he has done for his people, and yet, what is their response? Yep, you guessed it. They're not interested.

Re-engage

Jonah's main argument for not telling the city of Nineveh that they were going to be destroyed unless they changed their ways, was because he knew God would not destroy them in the end. Jonah knew that the disaster movie would end in peace and prosperity and not destruction – he felt the Ninevites weren't worthy of God's love...

>Why not write out verses 14–17 in your prayer journal and replace all the references to Israel and Jerusalem with references to yourself. Use it as a prayer whenever you need reminding that God has good things in store for you, and that there is a happy ending in the not-so-distant future.

Divine retribution

Decompress

'Dear Lord, be with me as I read your Word. Speak directly to my heart and soul, fill me with your love and empower me to do your will.'

Now read Obadiah 1:1-21

Immerse

We don't know anything about Obadiah apart from his name, which means 'servant of the Lord' and that he probably prophesied around 587 BC and the capture of Jerusalem by the Babylonians, if that is what verses 10-14 refer to.

>International politics – there I've said it. More than half of you have probably fallen asleep already. For those who are still awake, I'll continue. In theory, the United Nations can come to the help of countries who are either at war or being attacked. Unfortunately it doesn't always work like that, and quite often the bickering in the corridors of power stop any worthwhile intervention, leaving nations disunited and in harm's way.

>Edom had rejected God, which in itself was worthy of a little bit of divine wrath. But here they had also stood by while their close relative, Israel, had been plundered by Babylon (the even bigger bad boys). The words of Obadiah pronounce judgement, but also say that God will restore his people and everything will be put right in the end.

>Do we feel that we have been let down by others? How do we respond to it? Do we want to take matters into our own hands and serve the dish of revenge? Or do we lay it before God and let him deal with things?

Re-engage

Is there something that has upset you recently? Is there someone who you feel has let you down badly? Spend time telling God about and leaving it in his care. Why not write it on a piece of paper or in your prayer journal, and after telling God, get rid of the paper by ripping it out and throwing it away or even burning it (please be careful) to symbolically say that you have given it over to God.

Airlock: Dedicated

What dangers do we – the church –
face today which could cause
us to act in a prideful way and not
listen to God?

Extra_1 Proverbs 3:34
Extra_2 Romans 12:3

The divine treasure hunt

D/46

Decompress

'Forgetting the past and straining toward what is ahead, I keep trying to reach the goal and get the prize for which God called me through Christ to the life above.'
Philippians 3:14

Now read Matthew 13:44–46

Immerse

Jesus is nearing the end of a long sermon about 'the kingdom of heaven'. He is, as usual, speaking in parables – today's two parables deal with how much the individual will give up for the kingdom

>It's funny how whenever he preaches about heaven, Jesus avoids telling his disciples what it is really like. OK, so it might be a bit like a wedding feast, or a great banquet – but perhaps these pictures might just be metaphors for the real thing – only Jesus knows, and he didn't really give his disciples too many clues...

>So why does Jesus choose to spend so much time talking about the selection process as opposed to laying all the brilliance of heaven before our eyes? I think this parable may have the answer, although not in the way we would expect.

Re-engage

These are the sort of verses bandied about by the National Organisation of Smug Evangelical Christians demanding why we haven't given all of our inner beings unto the Lord, and why we persist in being grumpy in the morning and still shout at other drivers on the motorway.

>But have we really found the treasure yet? I'm not sure that Jesus expects everyone to stumble on the kingdom of heaven straight away, shout hallelujah and sing 'Hosanna!' in three-part harmony. This parable tells of the only possible outcome of finding heaven – complete and everlasting joy. If we haven't got that joy, well, maybe we should concentrate on the treasure hunt rather than on wondering whether other people have got to the treasure first. I'm sure there's plenty of treasure to go around, so get those trowels out and get digging!

>Obviously, there comes a moment in life where we realise a little bit more about what the treasure of the kingdom of heaven is, or at least find ourselves in the right field. Try talking to a more experienced Christian who you think has 'sold up' for Jesus and ask them why – it might give you some clues when treasure hunting...

Airlock: Dedicated

Something fishy…

Decompress

'… the voice from heaven spoke again, "God has made these things clean, so don't call them unholy"' Acts 11:9.

Now read Matthew 13:47–52

Immerse

In this parable, it is very clear that the task of judgement is not up to us. Everyone is included in the kingdom of heaven – Christian fish, Muslim fish, gay fish and alcoholic fish. God does the judging, not you, and the angels do the separating…

>Yes, we're back to fish again. But remember Jesus is talking to people who lived and worked near the Sea of Galilee. Notice how he uses an image that will appeal to his audience – an image that they will understand. It's so important to make sure that God's message is communicated in a relevant way to those who are listening – not to dilute the message, but to ensure that they are able to understand the truth behind the words. This is yet another answer to the question of why Jesus spoke in parables…

Re-engage

The final parable of this set is too often ignored by those Christians who would like to believe that Jesus was setting down immovable boundaries through his teaching. Jesus was reminding his contemporaries that his new teachings had to be incorporated alongside the 'old things' from the Old Testament. I believe that he was also warning future generations that there will be new challenges faced by the church, and not to be blinded to the new messages that the Holy Spirit guides them towards in order to help them deal with these new challenges.

>Many churches pride themselves on the 'new furniture' that has been purchased recently. In reality, however, we've gone through a period of restoring old furniture that has been hidden in the attic for many years. Feeding the poor, healing ministries, cell groups and worship leaders are all early church principles that somehow got lost over time, and have been rightfully restored to a central place in the modern church. The new role for women in the church is one example of new furniture, but I get the impression that there may be pressure for some more purchases on the way, with gay rights and a multi-faith society moving ever further up the agenda. And there's still lots of old furniture that needs restoring, and in some cases burning on the church bonfire…

Airlock: Dedicated

Not in my back yard

Decompress

'God knows that these things I write are not lies. In Judea the churches in Christ had never met me. They had only heard it said, "This man who was attacking us is now preaching the same faith that he once tried to destroy." And these believers praised God because of me' Galatians 1:20,22–24.

Now read Matthew 13:53–58

Immerse

I've changed quite a lot since I was at school. I shave my hair instead of gelling it. I eat more Italian food. I listen to Avril Lavigne and Shakira rather than the Carpenters. In fact, I have a completely different image now than Mr Geeky Acneface at school.

>Yet I always find it very difficult to accept that other people that I was at school with have changed as well. I'm sorry to say that I still cross over the road when I see people who were unkind to me back then, and I'm still scared of the adults who were once the school bullies. Beware! People can change…

Re-engage

Jesus must have been heartbroken by his reception in Nazareth. He had recently fulfilled his true vocation – and let's not forget how Jesus' life (as well as the rest of the world!) was changed by his baptism. Imagine you found you were able to save the world – where would you want to start?

>The hard-heartedness of Jesus' friends and neighbours in Nazareth is easy to understand, but we have to learn from it. It is not acceptable to judge someone on their past, because their present and future may be moving in a completely different direction. The inhabitants of Jesus' home town missed out on their salvation because they placed limitations on God's power. Yes, they probably did believe in the Messiah, but not in this manner and certainly not in their backyard.

>Do I believe God can change people? He's changed me, so I would have to answer yes. But it's sometimes difficult to have faith in people who have let us down before, particularly when we know that even people that God has changed aren't perfect. Think about how people you have known have changed. Are there people for whom you haven't accepted their new selves? Pray for God's help in this.

Airlock: Dedicated

Carry on kingy

Decompress

'Say only yes if you mean yes, and no if you mean no. If you say more than yes or no, it is from the Evil One' Matthew 5:37.

Now read Matthew 14:1–12

Immerse

Oh dear. Apparently Herod felt 'very sad' about cutting off John the Baptist's head, which makes all the difference. And it was a BIG mistake. You can imagine Herod looking over his shoulder all the time, knowing that he had been cowardly enough to kill a great prophet to appease his horrible wife, but not knowing whether his actions could come back and haunt him.

>Throughout the Bible, there are good and bad examples of leaders. Herod is a BAD example. What makes Herod a bad leader? Apart from the fact he is a murdering, hen-pecked, drunken cowardy custard? Well, compare this story with the story of David and Nathan in 2 Samuel 11,12. Both stories show leaders responding to criticism from prophets. But where David responds by admitting his guilt, Herod attempts to silence the prophet by locking him away.

>Herod cannot bear to be wrong because it detracts from his self-image of the all-powerful king. Herod, like Pilate later in the story, is shown to be a weak man who is trying to appease all sides, but gets it disastrously wrong. Sometimes there is room for compromise and for diplomacy, but there are other times that decisive action is needed. It is important in our relationships with others that we understand that sometimes someone might have to be upset in order for us to follow God's ways.

Re-engage

Sex and alcohol are two of the biggest thorns in the side for Christians. Most of us suffer from a partiality to one or the other of these at certain times in our life, and they can quite often lead us to make rash promises that we cannot keep. Pray for God's protection against two commodities that can be all very good in moderation but that can too often spiral out of control.

Airlock: Dedicated

Stop the world... ?

D/50

Decompress

'Jesus said to another man, "Follow me!" But he said, "Lord, first let me go and bury my father." But Jesus said to him, "Let the people who are dead bury their own dead. You must go and tell about the kingdom of God"' Luke 9:59,60.

Now read Matthew 14:13–21

Immerse

The feeling of bereavement is awful. Jesus' handling of his bereavement at the death of John is amazing. John the Baptist was his cousin as well as the man who gave him God's blessing in his mission. Jesus wanted to withdraw to a lonely place, no doubt to deal with his feelings privately, and to talk to God. But then he saw the crowd, who had walked for miles because they were trusting in him to free them from disease and oppression. And he pushed his feelings to one side, and put the people first…

>As ever, Jesus had an important reason for the miracle. He was particularly tired and emotional at this time, as we have seen. He had again poured himself out selflessly for the crowd, the people he had come to save. He was busily curing the sick,

comforting the hurting and making the blind see when…

>"Jesus, we're hungry and we haven't got any food."

>Jesus sees the perfect opportunity to get the disciples thinking beyond the material provisions of a situation and to use their faith. "Why don't you give them something to eat?"

>"Oh, but Jesus, we've only got five loaves and two fishes."

>"Yes, but if you do it like this…"

Re-engage

Don't get me wrong – I'm not suggesting that bereaved people should bottle up their grief and just get on with it. I'm sure Jesus wept more than just once in the Bible, and that he had plenty to say to his Father on the subject. But when one life ends, the rest of the world doesn't stop, as much as we would like it to. Pray for those who have recently died, that they might live on through the actions and works of those who have been bereaved.

A touch of your spirit (your spirit lives on)
I was lonely today, and I remembered your smile,
That made me feel special, that I was worthwhile,
And I wanted to hold you and I stretched my arms wide,
But I just hugged myself to keep the pain safe inside.

I was hurting today, and I wanted you near,
To help me release all the anger and fear,
And I wanted to hear you and I strained for your voice,
But I just heard the silence and I couldn't avoid
Crying out your name,
Just to hear it again,
To pretend you were still here with me.

But there's something about you,
That could not be destroyed,
For one touch of your spirit,
Released all your joy,
And where spirits united,
On my soul there's a mark,
And while I am still living,
Your spirit lives on in my heart.

I was laughing today, but the guilt carried on,
'Cos I shouldn't be happy now that your life is gone,
But I looked in the mirror, and I'm sure I could see
The familiar smile that you once smiled at me,
And I call out your name,
Just to hear it again,
For I know you are still here with me.

'Cos there's something about you,
That cannot be destroyed,
For one touch of your spirit,
Released all your joy,
And where spirits unite,
On my soul there's a mark,
And while I am still living,
Your spirit lives on in my heart.

© James Lovelock

Extra_1 Philippians 1:21–30
Extra_2 1 Thessalonians 4:13–18

Being hairy

D/51

Decompress

'God in heaven, show me what you want me to learn through this passage. Meet with me and speak clearly into my life!'

Now read Genesis 27:1–24

Immerse

What a story – it's got all the elements of deceit and envy that make for a good evening's entertainment in front of the telly. There's also an element of the bizarre – Jacob ends up with goat skins on his hands and neck – which goes to show that some people will go to any lengths for an inheritance! The ancient world believed that 'incredible powers' could be transmitted by blessings, and so Isaac had given Jacob this covenant blessing in a kind of legally binding way which makes the story such a big deal.

>Does this make you think about your family jealousy? Or does this draw out for you stuff about envy and wanting the skills or abilities or attention that is lavished on someone else in your family? My brother used to annoy me intensely by pretending I was better at our favourite sport of 'tree dangling' and then going inside, leaving me hanging there for hours on end as 'the winner'.

Airlock: Dedicated

Re-engage

What does this tell us about families and the way they work? Is there an issue here about respect for an older or younger sister or brother? How do you think this might change what you do next time you have a heated conversation with someone in your family – oh, and by the way, don't expect them to instantly respect you just because you are a Christian and you're doing what the Bible told you to do!

>Try this – email someone on your contacts list who isn't your favourite person in the world right now, family member or not, and tell them that they were uniquely made and God thinks they're amazing. Alternatively if you've had a falling out or a heated discussion with a family member or with a sibling recently, why not go and say sorry, and sort it out.

Being hairy (part 2)

D/52

Decompress

'Dear Lord, help me to learn valuable lessons about honesty and whatever else you can show me through the lives of these real people.'

Now read Genesis 27:25–45

Immerse

Switching the inheritance around is serious stuff, and this one act has repercussions that go throughout several chapters of these guys' histories. The name Jacob actually came to mean 'deceit' hence 'Jacob is the right name for him' in verse 36.

>In my family right now there's a similar thing going on – the inheritance of a family business has led to terrible anger and bitterness which has split one side of the family down the middle – sisters and brothers may never speak again as a result. It's really a horrible vindictive mess, in this case all because of people wanting to get their hands on some family money. And what good will that do them? The sad thing is that ultimately, it won't do them a lot of good at all.

Re-engage

Family ties can be very strong, but families can also be places where so much damage can be done to both relationships and to individuals.

>When there are difficulties at home, we need God's discernment in order to know what to do. Sometimes, it can be a matter of common sense, though. If there is a problem or an argument, what's the best thing to do – should you stay and try to sort it out there and then, when tempers are raised and anger is the emotion of the day, or should you step back and let everyone cool down a bit before trying to sort it out?

>Spend some time asking God to guide you through any difficult situations that you are facing at home. If your home life is going well, then pray, thanking him that things are going well. You could also pray for anyone you know who is having difficulties at home.

Parental Guidance

D/53

Decompress

'Speak to me about choice and relationships, Lord, because it's something I am facing at the moment. Help me to hear what you might be saying through this stuff, and help me to know how you want me to respond.'

Now read Genesis 27:46 – 28:9

Immerse

Some of the greatest stories ever written have been about love. Take Romeo and Juliet for instance. This tragic story of star-crossed lovers is built around the fact that their love is forbidden. Romeo and Juliet are not allowed to marry because of years of feuding by their respective families.

>Likewise, it looks like Jacob is having some restrictions placed on his roving – Rebekah basically has a problem with Hittite women, and so Isaac calls Jacob in and warns him about his choice of wife – he's only allowed to marry women from Canaan.

>Esau had been married at the age of 40 to two women who were daughters of Hittites, and we are told that they were a source of grief for his parents (Genesis 26:34,35). This shaped Rebekah's reaction, which is why she gets a bit anti-Hittite in her comments. So Jacob does as he's told and goes off to find a wife who is suitable for his parents..

Re-engage

What does this passage say to you about your parents'/carers' experiences and how they affect their advice to you? Do you think it was fair of Rebekah to say what she said to Isaac – knowing that he would inform Jacob and guide his choice of wife? Or is it true that she knew best after all?

>How about sitting down with your folks and asking them to describe their idea of a perfect wife/husband for you? I can remember my mum's words to this very day and I've had ten happy years of marriage so far and counting – although my parents are now divorced!

>If you can't bear talking to your parents, then put down a list of what you are looking for. But remember, you don't have to be looking for anything – being single (and yet still complete) is a respectable option to go for.

Airlock: Dedicated

Dreamtastic

Decompress

'God, help me to learn about how Jacob followed you, and how you spoke to him. I think there's something here about honouring your name, too, so please help me to learn about that.'

Now read Genesis 28:10–22

Immerse

God basically blasts Jacob's head through a dream – he shows him how powerful he really is, and gives him an incredible promise of inheritance. So many of the dreams I have are too wacky or mental for any kind of parallel here. But here God speaks in a powerful dream that shows that he is Lord of heaven and earth.

>The dream is so powerful that Jacob turns the stone he used as a pillow on its end and pours oil on it in order to make it holy – he is so awestruck that he basically commits himself to God all over again. He even renames the place Bethel (which means House of God).

>Dreams are used a lot in the Bible as a way of God communicating directly with people. Check out the stories of Joseph (son of Jacob, the one with the multi-coloured cloak, in Genesis 37) and of the other Joseph, (Mary's fiance in Matthew 18). Why do you think God used dreams like this?

Re-engage

Do you notice how Jacob is awestruck when God speaks to him through the dream – and how he reacts to it? Is this true of you? Do you ever kneel in surrender to God? Have you ever considered how totally awesome God is?

>How about a bit of exercise – kneel somewhere quiet, wait and listen to God, revelling in his awesomeness, praying.

>Is there somewhere on your journey to school/college/work where you could place a stone or rock like Jacob – so that every day, as you pass by it, you are reminded anew of God's love for you and his promise 'never to leave you'?

Don't try this at home

D/55

Decompress

You might like to view this passage in the context of those surrounding it – perhaps seeing some of the details here might give you a thought or two about your own relationships at the moment.

Now read Genesis 29:1–14

Immerse

This is a love story. Jacob continues his journey (remember that his father and mother have sent him out to find a wife). He has gone past Bethel, and now he reaches a field full of sheep. The shepherdess is rather attractive and Jacob snogs her after a slight conversation with other sheepy types about when to water the flocks.

>Although Jacob kisses Rachel, it probably wasn't in a way that we kiss someone we fancy (although there may have been an element of that in it). The primary motivation was because Jacob had met up with his uncle's family, and he was greeting a relation.

>What does this say about chance encounters and relationships? Do you find it a little confusing, or is it true to say that God destined it to be like this – an unplanned encounter with a shepherdess? I'll let you into a secret. It was an encounter like this that led to me getting married.

>If we trust our whole lives to God then we must expect the unexpected.

Re-engage

So what can we get from the story of Jacob and Rachel. Whatever you do, don't find a flock of sheep and snog the first person that comes along – but do take a risk, and ask God to be in charge of all your relationships. (Be warned, although Jacob ended up marrying Rachel, it took him seven years of hard work to move from initial kiss to wedding ceremony, and then a further seven years of hard work to pay off his uncle for the privilege of marrying her!)

>Think about past 'coincidences' in your life – have there been any? What would have happened if they hadn't happened?

Airlock: Dedicated

How do you think Jacob felt
when he awoke from his dream?
Do you think he ever doubted
God after this?

Extra_1 Psalm 77
Extra_2 Isaiah 7:10–17

Moment of truth

D/56

Decompress
Be prepared, be very prepared...

Now read Acts 8:1–8

Immerse
Aron Ralston, who comes from Colorado, loves the great outdoors. Earlier this year he was mountain biking in the mountains of Utah. He left the track to find a more challenging route, but was then trapped by a boulder that fell on both his arms. He managed to get one arm free, but the other one was stuck. By the following day he had finished all the water he had with him, and he knew that he faced a terrible choice – amputate his own arm or die. He made a tourniquet out of a pair of bike shorts but he only had a small pocketknife with him. It was so blunt that it took ages to even puncture his skin. He realised that there was no way he would be able to cut through his bone and so he worked out how to break his own arm. Having done that, it took him another hour to cut through the rest of his arm. He then set off to hike through the park and met some tourists who helped him find the helicopter that was searching for him. At the press conference after he was treated in hospital, he said he couldn't wait to get back to the mountains.

>Having started well, the early church now faces its moment of truth. Saul is so enraged by the faith of the new Christians that he unleashes a terrible persecution against the church. The new Christians literally have to run for their lives but look what happens as they do so.

Re-engage
Aron Ralston was faced with cutting off his own arm or dying. Having found himself in that situation, he made the choice that led to life and got on with it. None of the early Christians would have wanted persecution, but having found themselves under threat, they didn't hide – they told people about Jesus everywhere they went. Philip brought great joy to this city in Samaria, even though he knew that his brothers and sisters in Christ were being imprisoned and were suffering in other places. What would your reaction be?

>Find a snail in your garden and very gently poke it with a piece of grass – it will retreat into its shell. Ask God to help you respond to challenges to your faith like Philip, who talked about Jesus even though he knew it would get him into trouble, and not like a snail who hides at the slightest hint of danger.

Airlock: Dedicated

Only skin deep?

Decompress

It's time to look deep inside to see how deep your faith goes.

Now read Acts 8:9–25

Immerse

David Beckham is reported to have said that he definitely wanted to get his son Brooklyn christened, 'but I haven't decided into what religion yet.' I wonder what research he did, and how he decided? Maybe the one with the best theology of football, or the one that seems most cool? Or possibly the one that seems the most true?

>'Syncretism' means a blending together of different faiths in a pick-and-mix-tastic way without necessarily being aware that you are doing it. The Israelites in the Old Testament went through phases of worshipping other gods, such as Baal, and they needed the prophets to tell them they were wrong. Simon the sorcerer was like that even before he met Philip, blending his magic with enough of the Jewish faith to make people say his power was from God.

>Simon's conversion seems genuine in verse 13 – he's baptised and hangs round with Philip to discover more about this new faith. But when Peter and James show up, his actions show that, in fact, his conversion has not gone very deep at all. He treats them as if they were magicians and tries to buy this amazing 'trick' of filling people with the Holy Spirit, perhaps as the future finale of his show. Peter gives him an earful, and Simon realises his mistake.

Re-engage

How deep does your faith go? In many ways asking this question can stir up trouble. You don't need to get paranoid and question all your motives or actions: 'Did I really mean that prayer? What if I was accidentally not quite as sincere as I meant to be?'

>But it's also an important question to ask. Has every part of your life been touched by God, or are you keeping some things back? Are you a Christian in the way that you pray, or go to church, or read the bible – but when it comes to ambition, or future plans, or sex, are you any different to the people around you?

>Perhaps the most difficult areas for us to be consistently Christian are the old favourites of money, sex and power. Be brave and sit down with a friend to talk about the first one. Does your attitude to money match up with what Jesus said in Matthew 6:19–21?

Airlock: Dedicated

Severe Acute Real Spirituality

D/58

Decompress

How infectious are you? What do you pass on to the people around you?

Now read Acts 8:26–40

Immerse

Remember when super-virus SARS hit the news. Was it going to be a pandemic killing millions like the Spanish flu in 1918? Would it be as serious as AIDS? It spread to quite a few countries before people realised how serious it was, which is not surprising in these days of international travel. But what amazed me was how they were able to trace its spread through specific people who had been infected in one country and then travelled to another.

>In today's passage, we read of the start of the gospel spreading to 'the ends of the earth' as Jesus had said. Presumably this Ethiopian went back to his own country full of what had happened to him, as the people from different countries who had heard Peter preach in Acts 2 would have done.

Re-engage

This must be every evangelist's dream – to come across someone who is reading the Bible and who invites you to explain it to them. And who then wants to get baptised as you pass a handy pool.

>But it shows that God's spirit can be at work in surprising places. We may feel that we have to do all the work – praying, talking, caring for people, living out the gospel – and that's all really important. But sometimes it's the most surprising people in the most surprising places who are aware of God at work in their lives and need some help to understand what is happening. Would you have known how to answer the Ethiopian's questions?

>Write down the people that were involved in you coming to know Jesus. Pray for them and thank God that they played their part.

>Now ask God to show you where he is working in the lives of people around you. Keep your eyes open and prepare to be surprised.

Airlock: Dedicated

Saul-ophobia

Decompress

Who is the last person in the world you would expect to become a Christian?

Now read Acts 9:1–19a

Immerse

Have you seen any of those TV programmes where people are asked to conquer a phobia in order to win a massive prize? You get things like arachnaphobes having to put their hands in a bucket full of tarantulas, or people who are terrified of heights (or Acrophobes as they're known technically) climbing up the tallest ladder in the world

>This must have been the scariest thing Ananias had ever been asked to do. You can hear it in his reply to God. 'Don't you know what this man is like?'

>Look back at Acts 7:58, 8:1 and 8:3 to see what we already know about Saul. He watched and approved of Stephen's murder; he launched the persecution against the church and now he's taking it further, getting permission to persecute Christians in Damascus.

>Have you noticed a bit of a theme in these readings from Acts? God's spirit is at work doing incredible things but each time, he involves people. Sometimes it's a nice easy task like Philip and the Ethiopian; sometimes it's something incredibly scary like the things that poor old Ananias had to face. But God was with him and it must have been amazing to see Saul regain his sight and get baptised.

>Are you up for being involved in the work of God's kingdom – whatever it might be?

Re-engage

Write down the name of the friend that you least expect to become a Christian. Maybe they are quite outspoken in their criticism of Christians; or maybe they just seem totally uninterested. Pray for God to work in their lives by the power of his spirit. And keep on praying.

Mission impossible

Decompress

What proof do you need to see that someone has changed? Do you need to see it with your own eyes, or is it enough to hear about it?

Now read Acts 9:19b–31

Immerse

Imagine George W. Bush inviting Osama Bin Laden to stay at the White House for the weekend. It's pretty impossible, actually, but that's perhaps the scale of the turn-around that happened in Saul's life. From persecuting Christians viciously to preaching about Jesus. No wonder everyone in Jerusalem was so afraid of him.

>Having been so strongly against Christians, it's perhaps not surprising that Saul is now so strongly for Jesus, demolishing all the arguments against him and having threats made on his life. He doesn't seem the type of character who does things by halves.

>But he still needs a friend – someone who will stick up for him and introduce him to the church in Jerusalem. Later Saul, known as Paul, becomes key in the early church and in writing most of the New Testament, but we mustn't forget the crucial role that Barnabas plays in his life, supporting him and being there for him. Who could you be a Barnabas to – someone who encourages? Who has played that role in your life in the past?

Re-engage

Send a text message or an email, or even write a letter, to someone you know who is having a hard time at the moment. Tell them you are thinking of them and ask if there is anything you can do to help. Better still, arrange to meet up with them and go out somewhere for a long conversation and a spot of prayer.

>How important is it to be able to argue for the Christian faith like Saul did? Or is it more important to live a good life so that people can see you are a Christian? Which comes most naturally to you? Do you think everyone has the potential to be like Saul, explaining the Christian faith well? Or should we expect to have different gifts?

Airlock: Dedicated

The church now enjoys some calm
after the storm of persecution at the
beginning of Acts, but there are
many countries in the world where
Christians are still persecuted.
Have a look at the website of
Release International,
www.releaseinternational.org
an organisation that serves
persecuted Christians in over 40
countries around the world.

Extra_1 Lamentations 3:1–66
Extra_2 Lamentations 5:1–22

So sad

Decompress

Have you ever wished bad things would happen to someone, then felt sorry for them when they did? This is how Isaiah comes across as he recites God's verdict on Moab.

Now read Isaiah 15

Immerse

There were some horrible images published of the after-effects of the war in Iraq. Whatever your views on the politics of the matter, it seemed dreadful to most people that such terrible suffering had to be incurred by innocent civilians in order to obtain a regime change and to turn the country round.

>Isaiah has been speaking out these 'Messages to the nations' for two chapters now. They'll go on until chapter 23. He's done Babylon, Assyria and Philistia. In chapters 15 and 16 it's Moab's turn, a prophecy which is quoted and expanded in Jeremiah 48.

>As you read the passage today, you may well be amazed at the writer's unusual sensitivity concerning the suffering of an enemy – in this case the Moabites. See verse 5 in particular, where the prophet says, 'My heart cries with sorrow for Moab...'

Re-engage

Whenever we hear of God's judgement on sin in such harsh terms (and these are pretty harsh terms – check out the lions in verse 9!) it should encourage us to avoid all practices which the Lord finds detestable. I don't think we really have to list them all – you're probably already aware of what you ought to stop doing!

>Get out your prayer journal, and write down things you do which you know displease God on left-hand pages and good things you do on right-hand ones. Pray through each day's entries. Try and get it so that the lists on the right hand pages are longer than the lists on the left hand pages.

>Remember that person you started with in the Decompress section? The one you wanted bad things to happen to? Pray for them. Now. And, if you still see them regularly, pray for your attitude towards them – that your relationship would improve over the coming weeks and months.

Airlock: Dedicated

Big wrath, no grapes

Decompress

You want to pray but you just can't. Ever felt like this?

Now read Isaiah 16

Immerse

Big Brother, Survivor, I'm a Celebrity, Get Me Out of Here. All these reality TV programmes use deficiency as one of their main themes. Contestants are locked up in a house and deprived of some very basic things, or they're packed off to a desert island/the outback and have to fend for themselves. They normally have to undertake disgusting or difficult challenges to earn simple groceries and luxury items. The shows are designed so that the contestants begin to miss ordinary things from everyday life such as books, pens and paper, a hot shower and even clean clothes.

>As the Moabites flee from their country seeking refuge, they begin to lament the absence of their regular harvest of grapes and other ripe fruits. They remember the raisin cakes they made from the grapes. They remember the songs sung in the vineyards during harvest.

Re-engage

No one should expect Moabite gods to answer prayers (v 12 and see also Matthew 6:7). We should pray that God's Holy Spirit would help us to pray. Prayer is more than simply going through the motions of saying words. It's more than reciting words that we've learned off by heart. It's more than just shutting our eyes and talking to God. It's a conversation. It's two-way. There should be time for listening as well as talking. And we should pray in the expectation that God will answer our prayers - OK, he may not always answer them in the way that we want them answered, but he will answer them.

>Do you believe that? Do you trust that God will answer all of your prayers before you pray them? Or are you sometimes guilty of just shutting your eyes and praying into a void?

>Try to find out more about countries your own country often considers its enemies, or at least rivals. Read the foreign news pages of a newspaper today if you can.

Airlock: Dedicated

Ground force

D/63

Decompress
Some plants just won't grow in some places. Have you ever watched a member of your family (or indeed attempted yourself) trying to grow some fancy herb, vegetable or flower with spectacular failure?

Now read Isaiah 17

Immerse
The whole world of TV is infatuated with gardening programmes. And one of the things that has caused this outburst of enthusiasm is the idea that someone might come and do your garden for you. A free makeover. You see the world is divided into those who like gardening (about four people) and everyone else who is waiting for one of the people who like gardening to come round and do their garden for them for nothing. Gardening involves hard work.

>Imagine cultivating a magnificent garden but in the process so annoying the neighbours that they all decide to come round one night and trash it.

>Israel had been complacent, planting 'grapevines from faraway places...' whilst forgetting God's judgement. It would be conquered and nobody would be around to collect the harvest.

>This short oracle starts against Syria (capital Damascus) but soon moves on to Israel itself as the subject of the outburst. It suggests that it was spoken out at a time when Israel and Syria were allies.

Re-engage
Make an effort over the next few days to live each day without complacency – a day given to you as God's gift.

>Can you get involved in a local project to make your home city/town/village a more God-fearing place?

>Thorny question of the day: Old Testament judgement always seems to be visited on a nation by an opposing enemy army (Babylon, Philistia, Assyria etc). Since the New Testament, has it changed to become a more individual thing or might there still be judgement on a whole nation?

Airlock: Dedicated

Smoothies

Decompress

Take a moment to think about the things you are going to have to face in the near future which you are not looking forward to at all.

Now read Isaiah 18

Immerse

Is there something on the horizon that you are dreading – an exam, a hospital appointment, moving away from home for the first time. Can you see past it? Sometimes a big thing will 'loom up' in our near future and we see it out of all proportion. We cannot see round, or beyond this 'thing'.

>Our passage today has Ethiopia (Cush is what we know as modern day Ethiopia – their warriors had a fearsome reputation and had already taken control of much of Egypt) as the big thing looming large on the horizon for Israel. But Isaiah's oracle encourages his readers/hearers to see the more distant future. 'These people who threaten us will one day pay homage to our king', he says (v 7).

>Likewise this thing that's looming large on your horizon, the thing that threatens you at this precise moment, will one day contribute to making you the person you become, even though you will have to go through an experience that you dread beforehand.

>There is resurrection on the other side of the cross, but there is a cross. When things are really rough, hope helps you live with the present.

Re-engage

For everything that's coming up that fills you with dread, try also to focus on something else you are anticipating with joy. Focus your mental energies on the things you are looking forward to, and try not to think about the things which are worrying you. I know it's one of those things that's easier said than done, but try introducing the power of positive thinking into your life. Say, 'I am the best me there is.'

>Spend some time praying for yourself if there is something 'big' that you are having to face, or for someone else you know who is currently up against it.

>How can you encourage someone who says their life has no joy in it, and that they've nothing to look forward to?

Airlock: Dedicated

Stinking thinking

Decompress

No matter who you are, or how good you are at whatever it is you are good at, or how wealthy you are, or how safe you feel, God is watching over you.

Now read Isaiah 19

Immerse

The last time I went to a live football game, the home team were leading 1-0 going into the final five minutes. The away team were piling on loads of pressure, though, and a minute from the end, they scrambled a goal. The home team picked the ball out the back of their net and quickly kicked off. Some of the away players were still celebrating the goal, thinking the game was effectively over. Alas, the home team took advantage of their complacency, going straight down the other end from the kick off and putting the ball in the back of the net to win 2–1.

>Complacency is the curse of the effective. Egypt had everything – courage, plans, water, crops, fish, advisers, history and leaders. Yet none of these would be any use in the face of the Lord all-powerful. The message of this passage is to put God first. Write his name at the top of the top of the page.

>This passage goes beyond most Old Testament expressions about the fate of Gentile (non-Jewish) nations. It anticipates a day when Egypt will allow its people to worship God (v 21) and pray to him (v 22). This will also be a time when cooperation between Egypt, Assyria and Israel will take place naturally (v 24) and a day when each of those countries will acknowledge the one true God, as their creator (v 25).

>Although the Gospel to the Gentiles was not made completely clear until the Acts of the Apostles, it is previewed in this and other places.

Re-engage

However well you are doing, always find time to worship God and put him first.

>Thank God that, through Jesus, the price of sin has been paid. However many times you forget to put God first you can always start again without having to go through what the Egyptians had to suffer.

Airlock: Dedicated

'Careful what you do with that asherah, Trevor!'

Got any worthless poles, idols or altars you want to own up to? What are today's equivalents?

God owns us.

Really.

No, really.

Extra_1 Deuteronomy 6:13–15
Extra_2 Acts 17:16–34

Also available!

Look out for further books in the Airlock series:–

Airlock: Arrival
Airlock: Becoming
Airlock: Continuing
Airlock: Enthusiasm
Airlock: Future perfect
Airlock: Growing
Airlock: Heavenly

**Available from SU Mail Order on 0845 0706 006;
online at www.scriptureunion.org.uk/shop
or at all good Christian bookshops.**

(Non-UK users contact your national Scripture Union office.)